CHURCH MUSIC AND THE CHRISTIAN FAITH

Erik Routley

Foreword by Martin E. Marty

AGAPE
Carol Stream, Illinois 60188

```
   Third Printing  NOV 197ͻ
  Fourth Printing  JULY 1981
   Fifth Printing  JAN 1983
   Sixth Printing  OCT 1984
 Seventh Printing  DEC 1987
  Eighth Printing  JAN 1990
   Ninth Printing  AUG 1995
```

II

Foreword

When television cameras scan a crowd during the playing of the national anthem at athletic events, they can focus on only a very few lusty singers. Most of the audience merely lips the words, mumbles, chews gum, or waits for the music to end so the action can begin. If adult Americans do not sing at rites celebrating their nation, we can assume they rarely sing elsewhere. But there is one exception. Among those four out of ten citizens who worship each week, a large minority at least can be seen and even heard raising voices in song for the praise of God. The fact that the church can evoke a vocal response provides some sort of clue to the meaning of congregating and the value of music.

If some Americans treasure song enough to sing in the sanctuary, many of them also go one step further and fight about singing and song and then add still one more step by arguing also about instrumental music in the setting of worship. While church historians keep their chronicles on the relation between church and state and while journalists dutifully report on large ecclesiastical conventions, those who would faithfully account for the real hopes and fears of Christian people do well to pay attention to Sunday church bulletins, to read "Letters to the editors" columns of denominational magazines, or eavesdrop on congregational debates whenever someone suggests revision of hymnals, the hiring and firing of organists, or the use of guitars. Over such issues churches divide, ulcers develop, or, when there is harmony about harmony, true reconciliation emerges to provide new bonds between Christian people.

Far from deploring the fact of congregational singing, as the great writer C. S. Lewis inexplicably did, or ruing the fact that hymnody and church music can produce controversy, Erik Routley has made a career of celebrating the first fact and addressing the reasons for the second. He writes almost in the spirit of Alfred North Whitehead, who claimed

III

that a clash of doctrines is an opportunity, not a disaster. For Routley, the disputes about the role of music in the churches has to do with doctrines, with profound outlooks about faith and practice. Fortunately for readers, he is sufficiently opinionated to hold their attention just as he is more than sufficiently coherent in organizing those opinions so that they can understand the consistency of his own position. For him it would be less important that readers agree with him than that they would, as a consequence of paying attention, raise the level of their understanding and bring more civility and Christian reflection to debates now often based on mere passion and prejudice.

Church Music and The Christian Faith makes its appearance at a most difficult moment for church music. The Western Christian world has just experienced a decade of experiment occasioned by everything from the Second Vatican Council to the Counter Culture. For a time mere novelty seemed to be winning out until reaction set in, whereupon mere nostalgia for older forms sometimes has taken over. In the midst of the experiments some good things emerged, as the author of this book would be the first to agree. But the era left Christian people shaken and uncertain about values in the arts that they associated with worship.

Before the last overtones of the sixties had settled in the distant transepts, along came the seventies with a new set of problems for the church musician. Most notable among these is a generally welcomed populism in worship, a kind of seizure of power by a not always informed laity that has brought Country and Western into the sanctuary, reached for some of the more sensational effects of Gospel music, and reproduced in uncongenial and unfamiliar settings some of the music that grew up in the profound context of black worship. There have been gains as a result of this new "peoples' music," gains in the form of participation, immediacy, and a hold on emotions. The losses, from Routley's point of view—and I hope he convinces readers who have not thought about it before—can also be great. Much of the new music is, in his terms, romantic, sentimental,

IV

self-engrossed; it diverts from the true message of the Christian Gospel, however emotionally satisfying it may seem on the short run or the first hearing.

To bring up such subjects is not popular at the moment. The intrepid writer who puts them on the agenda runs the risk of being dismissed as an elitist or a snob. Erik Routley is aware that he may thus be condemned or, worse, shunned to the point of being ignored, and takes more pains than may seem necessary to show in what ways his approach in the end is also close to Christian people and is not purely the property of the experts. At the same time, he does defend certain kinds of theological and musical experts. In a world where if you do not know your furs you are advised to know your furrier or where if you do not know your jewels you should come to know your jeweler, people often fail to consult their musician or theologian when they do not know music or theology. Such consultation will not save souls, make all sad hearts glad, solve all problems, or lead to pure consensus. It should improve discussion and awareness, and that would be a boon in the Christian community.

To argue that matters of taste have something to do with the shape of God's action in Christ when the New Testament says so little about music and the arts is daring. To urge that our concepts of music should follow something of the trajectory of God's movement toward us seems beside the point to many of the people who genuinely share trust in that movement. Yet that is precisely what Routley sets out to do on these pages, not by presenting a formidable systematic work but by writing little prose exercises and figures, etudes and preludes, some of them marked *profundo* and just as many others light and tinged with grace notes.

Why bother with taste and why seek to produce our best in the context of Christian worship? Why bother in a time when it is vital to evangelize the world and urgent to feed it? A hint to the answer Routley provides is locked into a word that barely makes it into our dictionaries: *intrinsically*. If something is "intrinsic," it "pertains to the essential nature of a thing." Thus the value of a flower or its beauty is intrinsic; it need not exist for something else. Christians do not comfort people who suffer terminal illness with some extrinsic or ulterior value in view: because the person might survive and support a future stewardship campaign, or so that the church will be written into a will. The intrinsicality of their act is its only measure: that day there is comfort and love and these need no justification. Routley is concerned with the intrinsicality of appropriate music in the Christian context. He is likely to inspire thought among all readers, to jar a few, to convince many. If you are among the convinced, you might wish to sing an "Amen!" But I urge you to wait with even *that* word until you have read what he has to say on it. As for a "Hallelujah!" or two, no one will be holding you back.

Martin E. Marty
Fairfax Cone Distinguished Service Professor at
The University of Chicago

To
IAN MACKENZIE
with respect

AUTHOR'S NOTE

This is a complete revision of an earlier book of mine, called *Church Music and Theology*, published in 1959 by the S.C.M. Press in London. Not a page has gone unaltered, and nearly twenty years' further experience has caused me to express in a new way the convictions which inspired the earlier book. The theological background remains much as it was. I think I retain my beliefs, but what I now want to say about them is importantly different from what I wanted to say in the 1950s. I especially wish to record my gratitude to a host of American friends whom I have met during the past twenty years, and whose assistance, whether or not they knew they were giving it, has helped me see many things rather less obscurely than I did when I wrote the former book. So I invite the reader to forget the old one and, so far as it is possible, to enjoy this one.

ERIK ROUTLEY
Princeton, N.J.
1978

Contents

1

The Problem

Is Saul among the Prophets?

The earliest expression of the problem I plan to expose appears, I believe, in 1 Samuel 10. This chapter gives a startling and vivid picture of the wild religion which was a life-principle in the nation of Israel, and of the uneasiness with which ordinary people regarded it. Saul, selected to become the first king of a people disillusioned with the disorganized life they had led for generations under one popular leader after another, was told by Samuel that he would shortly have certain experiences which would prove that his selection was of divine origin. One sign would be practical—he would find a herd of cattle whose loss had caused his family some anxiety; the second would be charismatic—he would meet a group of men who would unexpectedly offer him a gift; and the third would be religious—he would meet a company of prophets and find himself able to prophesy with them. Thus he was to be convinced of his personal equipment for the task of being king and priest over Israel: he would have proof of his wits, his authority, and his mastery of the spiritual world.

Now the prophets of whom Samuel spoke were not preachers, but folk singers and dancers. And when Saul did indeed encounter a band of prophets at Gibeah, what he fell in with was a wild processional dance. They were, as Samuel had predicted, "coming down from the high place with harp, tambourine, flute, and lyre before them, prophesying." These prophets were very unlike the moralist-prophets of the later Old Testament books. They represented the people's religion in their singing and dancing associated with ritual sacrifices. They did not teach; they impersonated the supernatural.

It is written that when Saul joined in the dance it caused great surprise to the bystanders, who exclaimed, "What has come over the son of Kish? Is Saul also among the prophets?" In his commentary on Samuel, Dr. George Caird made this apt and epigrammatic observation:

> Whether the onlookers were surprised to find the unimaginative son of a farmer in the goodly fellowship of the prophets because they did not think he had it in him, or were shocked to see the son of a well-to-do landowner keeping such disreputable company, we can hardly say. . . . Prophets were religiously respected for their abnormal powers but socially despised for their uncouth ways, and on either ground Saul was in unexpected company.[1]

Therefore, says the writer of 1 Samuel, the saying "Is Saul among the prophets?" became a proverbial saying, meaning what we mean when we speak of a fish out of water.

One possible use of this story today makes the prophets stand for musicians and Saul for the Establishment. This can be any establishment you like—religious institutions, philosophical criticism, or even secular music. All of these establishments are easily tempted away from taking church music seriously, and in its presence they are either overbearing or uneasy. History agrees, for the most part, as I have attempted to show in my book *The Church and Music*. For present purposes the reader need only look at the contemporary church. Toward church music the establishment usually accepts one of two attitudes: a patronizing indifference, or a repressive dogmatism.

The chief offender in our time is probably not the hierarchy of any visible Christian denomination nor the reigning Pentagon of musical experts; still less is it secular philosophy. The establishment most to be feared, for its impatient scorn or its raised eyebrows, is the Christian congregation. This is natural in a day when words such as "participation," "communication," and "democracy" are widely used. It is public opinion which determines both what will prove practical in a

---

[1]George Caird, *The Interpreter's Bible*, Vol. 2 (Abingdon Press,), p. 934.

church and what will bring a publisher a good return on his outlay. If the establishment insists that Saul would be wiser to abandon his vision and keep clear of prophetic ecstasies, it will eventually achieve the suicide of Saul (as in the story) and the relapse of the society it controls into aimless but comfortable mediocrity.

Whatever is said, then, in an attempt to find a theological basis for judging and using church music must be said against this stream of popular "establishment" opinion. At the same time it is quite useless to proceed on the assumption that even Saul himself can do without theological principles. Theology, for our purposes, is speech about God and his ways. On that assumption theology cannot be irrelevant to any consideration of music designed to assist in the worship of God. Even if church musicians' ecstasies are now more organized and less esoteric than those of Saul's prophets, they nonetheless have a right not only to the craftsman's freedom but also to be taken seriously and to have their best expected of them.

We shall therefore look for some means of reconciling these phrase-making bystanders with the prophetic vision and of helping them to accept the new kind of Saul. Saul can no longer be regarded as merely the representative of popular opinion, any more than he can be regarded as merely a singer or dancer. He is, or rather must give place to, a King who reigns over both the worlds of reason and of vision. Since the New Testament tells us in precise terms who and what that King now is, we ought to be able to move on with confidence.

Some Presuppositions

This leads us at once to an important preliminary statement. We live in the days of the New Testament, not the Old. Therefore we must not be tempted to look in the Old Testament for precise instructions on what everybody should always do or judge right and good. The pattern "Saul-prophets-bystanders" is a typically Old Testament pattern. Saul was, or was about to be, a king; the prophets were

3

religious instruments, respected for their abnormal powers. In the Old Testament, the distinguished is always abnormal. "The spirit" was a gift which few were allowed (but it was present in the prophets and in Saul when he joined them). The New Testament assures us of the right given to all to become sons of God, of the universal dissemination of the Holy Spirit. It is never right to assume that the Spirit will not appear in public opinion, but will exclusively manifest itself in some levitical caste of musicians or priestly caste of theologians.

We can neither look for a Samuel to make our decisions for us, nor escape the necessity of extracting from history and contemporary movements guidance on how to make those decisions. If the following pages are to be both theoretical and practical, they must avoid being either fugitively dogmatic or passively complacent about popular tastes. We have just passed through a period when pedagogy in church music, although it did a necessary piece of work, proved a shade "Old Testament" and oppressive in its manner. But we must try to do better than simply let things slither into a totally permissive pattern. For the New Testament truth is not that all laws of behavior are abrogated by Christ, but rather that a Kingdom has been manifested in which what is right is also what is wholly delightful. Where there is no right, therefore, neither is there any pleasure that lasts. Human nature is not constructed to operate in a moral vacuum; it ought to be evident that there is a condition which is neither bondage nor vacuum, but felicity. It is toward this august end that we presume here to encourage movement. What theology ought to be able to achieve is not so much the establishing of laws as the removing of taboos, embarrassments, and barriers to decent conversation. This is what the New Testament is about.

So biblical evidences must be considered; but the Bible is sterile until it has chimed with human experience and personal conviction. Musical conventions and teachings must be investigated, but, as we shall see, these can become a pharisaic law administered by people who can neither make music nor permit others to make it. Strictly practical things about which ordinary people in Christian institutions have to make decisions must be dealt with, but in an exemplary rather than a didactic fashion. History is full of well-meaning church people who have tried to guide musicians but have succeeded only in making judgments which no musician could accept and remain a musician. Where these judgments have been inadequate, whether it was John Wesley's disapproval of vocal polyphony or a papal interdict on the use of pianos in church, this has been because the law became in their hands pharisaic: the letter was lethal because the spirit had been ignored or forgotten. But, in fact, often the letter did not kill, because the musician continued to be undemonstratively disobedient. The consequent situation was, if not as bad as it might have been had musicians accepted literally the pronouncements of their superiors, still uneasy and unproductive of friendly relations between theology, or church establishment, and music.

2

The Old Testament

Singing to the Lord

It is in the nature of things that people should want to "sing to the Lord," and the practices associated with religion in Old Testament times share with those of all religions in making provision for man's response to this commandment of natural law. The injunction "Sing to the Lord," so characteristic of the Psalmists and other singers (e.g. Ex. 15:21; 1 Chr. 16:9; Ps. 68:32; 96:1,2; 98:1; Isa. 42:10; Jer. 20:13; etc.), is less a demand for specific action than a signal that what has been waiting for expression may now be given it.

The history of biblical music is well summarized in Chapter VII of the *New Oxford History of Music*, Vol. I. I need not recapitulate the story here. It is worth noting, however, that these authorities leave us in no doubt that the Scriptures (our only source of knowledge about the music of Israel) are in themselves a secondary, unreliable, and almost accidental source. That is not surprising. The last thing to occur to a Jewish writer under the Old Covenant would have been to write a history of music. Music was to him so natural an activity as to be hardly susceptible at that stage of moral criticism. (Moral criticism of music in the Old Testament is, as we shall see, always criticism of the musician.) All we can gather from the Old Testament is that music was in very wide use in the culture of Israel at all its stages, from the primitive triumph song of Miriam to the relatively sophisticated liturgical system of the Second Temple, and that this music was always sung and frequently accompanied by musical instruments. The nature of these instruments is, apart from the most generalized classifications, purely conjectural, and our opinions on it are based on no archeological or historical evidence whatever.

As for the music itself, we can distinguish epics and dirges in secular contexts (insofar as any context for Israel was secular), and songs of praise, thanksgiving, instruction, personal experience, and liturgical significance in the religious context. Professor Sigmund Mowinckel has taught us of the august liturgical import of the Enthronement Psalms. The text of the Psalms of Ascent gives ground for a clear reconstruction of the half-domestic, half-open-air context in which they were used. Linguistic evidences combined with attention to their content show us with reasonable plausibility the source of certain reflections on personal experience or on history, such as we find in Psalms 129 or 137. Certain sidelights are thrown on popular musical habits by the appearance of a lyric such as that which opens Isaiah 5. All this, with other studies of a similar sort, indicates that music was never far from poetry, and poetry was never regarded as wholly irrelevant to the imparting of that religious conviction which is the chief business of the Old Testament.

The Axis of Old Testament Criticism

It is quite clear—indeed, given any understanding of the sacred writers' purpose in the Old Testament, it is clear *a priori*—that while any conclusions based on Scripture concerning the history of pre-Christian music are bound to be highly conjectural, the Old Testament is an excellent source for moral teaching about its religious use. Here the Old Testament evidences are as clear and persuasive as their historical evidences are hazy and accidental. One does not read the Old Testament to ascertain facts of natural history, nor read fiction in order to be informed about railways. What the Old Testament is concerned with is the revelation given by God to his people, and the category within which this revelation is most often transmitted is that of morals. God's will and man's rebellion is the normal polarity of Old Testament narrative, exhortation, or song. Along these lines we may be certain of finding guidance.

There is, then, an assumption that religious men and women respond to a call to sing to the Lord. This assumption corresponds to the natural desire to sing which, being as natural as the desire to speak, and quite possibly more primitive, is in itself morally neutral. Comment on this appears explicitly in certain places in the prophets, by way of warning people against the unrestricted or disobedient concessions that can be made to this non-moral desire. The moral content in "It is a good thing to give thanks to the Lord, to sing praises to thy name, O Most High" (Ps. 92:1) is of the lightest. Nobody ever thought it was a bad thing. But the prophets now and again comment on religious music making as characteristic of those habits of worship which bespeak a degenerate spiritual condition. The most unequivocal denunciation of religious music thus abused is in Amos 5:23–24:

> Take away from me the noise of your songs;
>   to the melody of your harps I will not listen.
> But let justice roll down like waters,
>   and righteousness like an ever-flowing stream.

This is almost paralleled, though not with respect to the musical reference, in Isa. 1:12–17 and Jer. 7:1–7.

More numerous are prophetic denunciations of music as a symbol of secular triviality. Amos in one place audaciously introduces the name of David in such a context:

> Woe to those who lie upon beds of ivory,
>   and stretch themselves upon their couches,
> and eat lambs from the flock,
>   and calves from the midst of the stall;
> who sing idle songs to the sound of the harp,
>   and like David invent for themselves instruments of music;
> who drink wine in bowls,
>   and annoint themselves with the finest oils;
>   but are not grieved over the ruin of Joseph! (Amos 6:4–6)

and Isaiah similarly:

> Woe to those who rise early in the morning,
>   that they may run after strong drink,

who tarry late into the evening
till wine inflames them!
They have lyre and harp,
timbrel and flute and wine at their feasts;
but they do not regard the deeds of the Lord,
or see the work of his hands (Isa. 5:11-12).

From such passages we can infer in their writers an acute
sense of the moral force of music. It was natural to them to
seize on its symbolic properties, and to reflect in their denunciations a truth which Plato expressed in more measured
terms in the *Republic* when he denounced certain musical
modes as agents of moral corruption.

Perhaps the single text in the Old Testament that reveals
what would now be called musical sensibility is Ezek.
33:32,33, where the inattentiveness and sentimentality of
the people toward the prophet's message is compared with
the attitude of people who listen to a sweet voice and a
seductive tune. Concertgoers who affect a certain kind of
beatific smile and gushing comment, the bane of sensitive
performers, are just what Ezekiel is thinking of.

But the critical reader will rightly urge us not to lay too
much weight on texts of this kind. After all, the passages
from Amos and Isaiah just quoted were written in Hebrew
poetry, and may well have been actually sung. By implica-
tion, the rebuke against the corruption of music is uttered in
sorrow against a *corruptio optimi*. Music ought not to be an
abomination, but it is made so by the repulsive incongruity
between its beauty and religious zeal and the state of things in
the city slums.

What really matters to us is the moral content of that law
which early Israel regarded as God's moral self-revelation to
his people. Not specific rebukes, but the principle behind all
Old Testament rebuke is what we must discover if we are to
use the Old Testament scriptures as a guide.

Now there is a tendency in most pious Christians, encouraged by a misreading of certain familiar passages in the
Gospels, which encourages the belief that a Christian can
gain little edification from the Jewish law. The Pauline
doctrine of the law as a dispensation from which a man "in

Christ" is released is never at any point so expressed as to mean that the law written in the early books of Scripture is to be disparaged; nonetheless, Paul is often regarded as authority for disparaging the law in Exodus and Leviticus. The same comment applies to the Epistle to the Hebrews. Above all, it most certainly applies to Matthew 5. Here a causal recollection of the chapter suggests to many people that our Lord said, "The law told you this; but I, contradicting it, tell you the opposite." Not at all.

Law and Gospel

The great series of antitheses in Mt. 5:21–48 are thus introduced:

> You have heard that it was said to the men of old, "You shall not kill..." (v. 21).

> You have heard that it was said, "You shall not commit adultery" (v. 27).

> You have heard that it was said to the men of old, "You shall not swear falsely ..." (v. 33).

> You have heard that it was said, "An eye for an eye..." (v. 38).

> You have heard that it was said, "You shall love your neighbor and hate your enemy" (v. 43).

Of these, the first three contain quotations from that summary of moral law which we call the Ten Commandments (Exodus 20). Our Lord's comment in each case is that mere avoidance of error, or of technical breach of the law, is an insufficient aim for his disciples. The fourth is a quotation from Ex. 21:24, a passage susceptible of much critical comment. The immediate context of this application of the *lex talionis* is the highly specialized case of injury sustained by a pregnant woman in consequence of a brawl; but commentators are prepared to say that although it appears at this point, it is applicable to all the cases of injury mentioned in

10

the preceding verses. Whatever may be the truth about the text, it is difficult to suppose that our Lord in speaking, or the evangelist in reporting and collating several of his speeches, would pass so abruptly from precepts of universal application to a comment on one fairly remote clause in the statutes of ancient Israel. Obviously what he means is, "Your habit of thinking is, 'an eye for an eye, a tooth for a tooth.'" He flatly denies this habit of thinking in a manner in which he does not flatly deny the quotations from the Commandments.

The transition to the fifth clause then becomes quite smooth. "You shall love your neighbor" does indeed stand in Lev. 19:18. But "you shall hate your enemy" stands nowhere in Scripture. What our Lord here directly denies is, again, a common habit of thought. If any law of the land were based on it, he would deny that as well; but the point here is that he did not deny the law as written in Scripture. With all his force he denied the pharisaic and popular interpretations of it, and with all his force he emphasized the necessity of doing more than merely avoiding breach of it. But in the law as his fathers according to the flesh understood it, in the law as God's moral self-revelation, he never saw anything but an object of veneration.

We have already suggested that the essence of Christ's moral teaching is that it is not enough to be blameless, that blamelessness will not save. And that, as we shall see, is a cardinal point in our present argument. But it is worth our while to observe one more way in which the Old Testament can enlighten us before we fully take into account the New Testament.

The Principle of Restraint

Although it must be agreed that the old law is expressed largely in the form of prohibitions, it cannot have escaped a careful reader of the law that it is unlike any other legal system in its ruthless abhorrence of human pride, self-sufficiency, and meanness. Much of the law, of course, contains rough justice of the kind that to some extent persists in modern society. The death penalty is appointed for crimes of which murder is only one (though murder is distinguished, in Ex. 21:12ff., from other kinds of killing). A domestic life, a view of marriage, is presupposed from which we may fairly say that Christianity has delivered us. And yet consider such injunctions as these:

> If you meet your enemy's ox or his ass going astray, you shall bring it back to him. If you see the ass of one who hates you lying under its burden, you shall refrain from leaving him with it; you shall help him to lift it up (Ex. 23:4–5).

> When you reap the harvest of your land, you shall not reap your field to its very border, neither shall you gather the gleanings after your harvest. And you shall not strip your vineyard bare, neither shall you gather the fallen grapes of your vineyard; you shall leave them for the poor and for the sojourner: I am the Lord your God (Lev. 19:9–10).

> When you make your neighbor a loan of any sort, you shall not go into his house to fetch his pledge. You shall stand outside, and the man to whom you make the loan shall bring the pledge to you. And if he is a poor man, you shall not sleep in his pledge [i.e. the coat which is the only pledge a poor man can offer, and which serves him also for a blanket]; when the sun goes down, you shall restore to him the pledge that he may sleep in his cloak and bless you; and it shall be righteousness to you before the Lord your God (Deut. 24:10–13).

The second passage chimes sympathetically with another (Ex. 23:10–12, cf. Lev. 25:1–7) in which the Israelite is commanded to plow and sow his land for six years, and for the seventh to allow it to lie fallow "that the poor of the people may eat" (Ex. 23:11). This is called in Lev. 25:6 the "sabbath of the land." Despite the august association of the sabbath in Exodus 20:11 with the finishing of creation, its social importance lay in its inducing a habit of desisting not only from work as onerous, but also from work as profitable.

"This shall be righteousness to you before the Lord your God." This technique of self-restraint, implying self-abasement, is what will, says the sacred legislator, put you right before God and enable you to share responsibility in God's design for the world. It is hardly too much to say that behind this precept is the notion that this self-restraint in mankind is the only thing that corresponds to the self-restraint which is God's own technique in creating and bearing with the world.

It can further be said—and indeed I here propose to treat it as settled—that when our Lord resisted the law, he was primarily resisting those interpretations of it which had drained off from it this irrigation of generosity. He was attacking those disciplines which, having lost the saving aim of mercy, were now nothing but means to that very pride which was the law's primary target.

It is recognized from the earliest stages of religious consciousness in the Old Testament that the archetypal sin is pride. In ordinary practice the defense against this sin is the principle of restraint, the principle that you have no proved right to all that is lawfully yours. All the Old Testament morality could be arranged along this one axis, that you must renounce part of what you are entitled to. There is a direct line from Leviticus 19 to Philippians 2. Indeed, the hither end of that line is to be found earlier than Leviticus: in Genesis 14, where Abraham learns at the hand of Melchizedek to renounce his lawful spoils of war; and on the earliest pages, where God permits his creatures to exercise independent judgment and choice. In these places we have a negative and partial expression of that total and positive doctrine of grace on which all New Testament teaching so firmly insists.

This principle already states that corresponding to God's limitation of his omnipotence is a freedom in his creatures to love him, or to hate him, by choice. Derived from that in the Old Testament is the creature's primary moral duty to renounce his tithe. If, then, a creative faculty in the creature corresponds in any way to the creative act in the Creator, we, who can never create *ex nihilo* but only in manipulating material which God has made, are called to renounce what corresponds to the absolute omnipotence that God renounced. If we believe that God's omnipotence is limited in order to make possible a rational and living creation, we must believe that an artist's rights over his "creation" are similarly limited.

Certainly we hold that between human beings the exercise of absolute omnipotence is a blasphemy. That is tyranny, and on whatever scale it is exercised we hold it to be evil. History insists that tyranny does not produce a rational and healthy society, even though history's lessons are not easily or quickly learned by history's children. Israel under Ahab was not more rational and healthy than it was under the judges, when there were so many periods of anarchy. But the Old Testament takes us only so far. It demonstrates in dozens of different ways the two dangers between which a human society constantly travels: the danger of anarchy and that of tyranny, or the evil of acknowledging no authority and that of being compelled to acknowledge a tyrannous authority. The secret of maintaining the needful dynamic equilibrium is what the New Testament spells out.

3

The New Testament

The Ethic of Grace

When we turn to the New Testament we find no reference to music, apart from certain heraldic references in the book of Revelation to the singing of the heavenly hosts, and a stray remark in two of the Epistles about the singing of hymns and spiritual songs (Col. 3:16; Eph. 5:19). Although there is no instruction in the New Testament on this subject, there are principles. What chiefly concerns us here is the principle of grace as distinguished from the principle of law.

In *The Gift of Conversion*, I attempted to identify this principle and demonstrate to the best of my ability that the principle of grace is implicit in the Old Testament and explicit in the New. It is exposed in the discourse of our Lord which St. Matthew records in Chapters 5-7. At the opening of that discourse our Lord says clearly, "Do not suppose that I have come to abolish the law and the prophets. I did not come to abolish, but to complete" (Mt. 5:17). The law, looked at from one point of view, says that blamelessness, if it can be achieved, is sufficient. Our Lord insists that blamelessness will not save. This is made plain in the teaching of Christ, which distinguishes between two worlds: that where the best one can achieve is the avoidance of error, and that where, avoiding error as a matter of course, one aims for an infinite extension of positive good. It is error, according to a law current in Christ's time, to go less than one mile with the man who obliges you to carry his pack. Going the second mile (Mt. 5:41) is more than a repetition of the first. It is a different kind of action which may well be met by a startled acceptance of your act of *grace*, where, had you gone only the first mile, you would have had a routine acceptance of your obedience to the law. I would thus summarize the New

Testament principle of grace:

1. Grace refers to a whole dimension of living, of which the "second mile" is an illustration.

2. The notion of grace is diversified over the whole range of human activity and consciousness, until it is fully understood that the state of Christian living in the Kingdom is a state I have described as "welcoming the duty." That is, without any abrogation of the person's right and duty to make free moral choices, what the person under grace wants and what God wills are in the end the same. Therein lies the blessedness (Mt. 5:3–12) or happiness which a person in Christ may legitimately seek and find.

3. It is God's design that the whole universe live consciously under grace; that the obedience we owe God in the moral field be reflected in all other fields, including the physical; and that our cheerful, chosen obedience to God result in a loving, self-restrained dominion over those things which in the natural order have been placed under our control. Such an attitude will evoke from them a similar cheerful obedience to us. This is the secret of Christ's own dominion over things during his incarnate life, which is exactly of the same kind as his dominion over people. Following Christ's pattern, to take a simple example, the disciple neither abuses his own body nor allows himself to worry about his health. Quite clearly Jesus did neither. Toward such a consummation, Christians believe, the "whole creation groans and travails."

4. Therefore, in the Kingdom, human beings are unconcerned with the kind of judgment (Mt. 7:1) that is faultfinding, because it makes the law their judge instead of their tutor. Living on the principle that judgment is faultfinding, a person will have, and will engender in others, a vision of God as a faultfinding judge, an examiner on the watch for mistakes (Mt. 7:2). It is for this reason that Jesus does not give short answers about the rules of the Kingdom. He tells us only the kinds of things we may expect to happen. He gives pictures, not precepts. True, certain primitive notions of practical justice are upset, as in the parable of the laborers in the vineyard (which is not a directive for economists but a picture of the surprises grace can provide). But this does not

imply that the law has disappeared. A citizen of the Kingdom is not allowed to commit adultery or murder. But then he doesn't want to; what he wants is to generate as much love as possible, not merely to avoid adultery and murder.

Instead of saying that this suggests a new style of aesthetic criticism, I contend that this is the unsuspected paradigm of all such criticism. Serious musical criticism has always taken for granted the fulfillment of the law, and gone on to assess how much positive good is achieved in this composition or that performance. How often a criticism will state: "A correct performance, lacking just that extra ounce of inspiration"; how often a reviewer finds himself hard put to devise a way of saying without offense, "This new anthem is blameless but screamingly dull."

It is obvious at once that this is the world in which the artist moves. That which distinguishes art from whatever one can call its opposite (the absence of a word for its opposite is itself a signal that we are moving in the new world) is analogous to that which distinguishes grace from its opposite. It is characteristic of New Testament thought, as we find it in this classic summary of Christ's teaching, that the opposite is an "absence." The artist in words, music, painting, or any other discipline is not avoiding error but seeking an extension of goodness. It must then be the basis of our argument that criticism about music, including church music, finds its natural form of expression within the New Testament world.

Standards

We can arrive at this principle from another direction by attending to what appears on the surface to be a more difficult passage, Gal. 3:1–5:1. This is the heart of an argument upon which the whole contention of this magnificent and angry document is based. We shall translate it into an argument about standards. It can be summarized as follows:

St. Paul is concerned that his friends in this Christian group (usually thought to be an ethnically unusual group, possibly of Celtic connections, in what is now northern

17

Turkey) have been seduced from the gospel at an early stage by somebody's presentation of a false faith. Paul says in his introduction (1:12) that the gospel he preaches was no human invention, but was received "through a revelation of Jesus Christ." He establishes at once the newness of the world in which his mind, as well as his spirit, moves. Pausing to offer an illustration of the difference between his two worlds, his analogy is that of an inheritance. The thing he wants to communicate is something promised by God to the first human being (according to the Old Testament scheme) who was capable of understanding it. This was Abraham, and Abraham turns out to be important. It was something far more than a guide to morality. It was the law, which is something intelligible to anybody, not something too precious to be entrusted to anyone but Abraham.

Faith, Paul continues, is older than and superior to law, and it brings us into a relationship with God which can be described by comparing the status of a son with that of a slave, of which the relationship between Christ and God, manifested to us in the incarnation, is the final sign (3:26–4:7). He breaks off to point out that the flat legalism of the Galatians' religious practice is a direct denial of this (4:8–11), and to beseech them to return to the faith he had preached and to set aside that which more attractive preachers, offering an easier way of life, had offered (4:12–20).

After all this he comes back to his argument and introduces the point which is especially useful for our purposes. He is back now with the slave/son distinction, and to illustrate it he takes an actual incident from the life of Abraham (4:21–5:1). Abraham, he reminds his readers, was, like all the patriarchs, polygamous. The fact that he had two wives, Sarah and Hagar, has no moral content. At least, it was not supposed to have. But there was, he tells them, that strange and sad incident which climaxed the feud between those two women. As Genesis records (21:1–10), Sarah at last lost patience and forced Abraham to turn out Hagar, the slave woman, and her child. Her jealousy insisted that Hagar be removed from her sight.

What Paul makes of this story is the proposition that although law (or what passed for it in those days) ordained that Abraham's having a child by Hagar was legitimate in view of Sarah's supposed barrenness, it was not at all what God had in mind. From the higher point of view this situation was all wrong. God's purpose was to be achieved through Sarah, and she and her husband had to learn through experience that they must wait for it, not bypass it by relying on what was merely legitimate. It may be added here that this same point is made in that equally symbolic story of Jacob. We are told that Jacob legitimately had four wives, but that not only was the tribe of Israel to be generated through Rachel, but also Rachel actually did mean more to him than did the others (in this case one was a free woman and two were slaves). The principle of monogamy seems to be foreshadowed from the beginning of the Old Testament—not precisely the legal principle of monogamy, but rather what we are content to call the kind of love that can exist only between one man and one woman. Not monogamy but love is what obstinately breaks through the pattern of the primitive society.

Sarah *meant* something totally different from Hagar. (More explicitly, Rachel *meant* more than the others.) In what sense did Sarah mean more? Well, says Paul, it is the difference between the two worlds we are speaking of. He brings in another analogy. Here is earthly Jerusalem, the capital city, the seat of government, the location of the Temple—a human city. Somewhere, we agree, is a heavenly order we are already calling the heavenly Jerusalem—a picture of the new world as a new city. Anybody could tell you, Paul implies, the difference between the geographical Jerusalem and the ideal city that is in the mind of God. Compare the two Jerusalems, compare the Sarah story with the Hagar story, or compare the son with the slave. That is the difference between faith and works, or grace and law, or the gospel of Paul and what the Galatians had been hearing from cheap preachers.

This brings us to the same point we reached in studying Matthew 5–7. It is, indeed, the gospel of liberation, in which

God's creatures are no longer children but adults (that point is made in Heb. 5:12–14) and must distinguish between the true gospel and false preaching.

We now have some useful guides for judging church music. On the one hand we have the principle that it is not the avoidance of error but the generation of good that we are to look for. On the other hand we have the principle that the Christian's goal must be maturity in Christ. Our Lord could not have been clearer about this, but Paul found constantly (as apparently did other teachers in the apostolic age) that to fallen human nature the status of the slave is attractive, while that of the son is demanding. The prodigal son, we remember, was not permitted by his father, despite his bad record, to take the job in the kitchen he asked for. He had to wear the robe and the ring and like it. Paul's great bugbear was circumcision, which people were trying to insist was a requirement for becoming one of Christ's people. Every time he meets it (as in Galatians) Paul is moved to olympian wrath. That, he always says, is exactly the sort of thing that destroys any hope that people will apprehend the gospel and lay hold of the liberty and responsibility of discipleship. We are therefore on firm ground in saying that where church music inhibits the growth of the Christian society to maturity it is to be censured. These two points are the chief contentions of what follows.

4

The Law and the Musician

At this point let us turn back and relate what we have said to the work of the musician. Let us ask first, to what does the law correspond in the musician's scheme? By law we shall mean what Paul meant by it and what Jesus meant as he is recorded in Matthew 5–7. We shall also remember that the law was regarded by the faithful in Old Testament times as something much more than a series of instructions designed to keep the peace and regulate life. We shall not leave Sinai out of consideration, nor the affection in which the author of Psalm 119 held the law. For that psalmist it was always "thy law," God's self-revelation to humanity, and humanity's best means of entering into God's confidence. There are two sides to it, and when Paul and Jesus speak of the law as something less than the perfect way of life they are referring to that misapprehension of it which caused people to reject Christ, who was in his own person the law's perfect fulfilment.

Consider then the law as tutor (Gal. 3:24). A musician who is learning his trade is taught that certain things are to be avoided. A student invited to harmonize a simple phrase might produce the following result:

The teacher would reprove the student for writing what are technically known as parallel fifths and octaves at the point marked. That, he would say, is wrong, and he would probably indicate several ways of harmonizing the passage which would avoid the error. The following are examples but do not by any means represent the full number of "correct" ways of working this exercise:

In what sense was the student's version wrong? The only answer is that it is ugly, or that it has an absence of the virtue proper to four-part music. The situation is illuminated when we ask in what circumstances parallel fifths or octaves are agreed not to be wrong at all. Here are some such situations.

1. In very primitive polyphonic music they were not wrong but right. A very early form of organum, found in vocal music of the fourteenth century, consisted of one part following another fairly faithfully at the interval of a fifth. It did not sound, and was not then considered, wrong at all. To modern ears it sounds quaint, if you like, but not ugly.

2. The following passage in a piece of music written about 1920 also does not sound, and is not judged to be, wrong:

3. In the music of Vaughan Williams one often comes across passages like the following, from his Mass in G Minor:

4. In a motet written in 1953 and thought to be one of his most exquisite pieces, the same composer wrote this:

Example 1 is based on the principle that the octave and the fifth are the first two harmonics of any fundamental note. It is natural, if a primitive musician wishes to pitch any note other than the one he is hearing, to light on the octave first, then the fifth. Also, vocal polyphony was more or less discovered because one kind of male voice has a range very roughly a fifth above the other kind. What began as a merely prudential device became, in course of time, a discovery in its own right of the possibilities of voices singing different parts. As soon as this was fully revealed, it became clear that much more music could be made if two, three, or four parts moved independently. Where two parts move at the interval of an octave or a fifth they abandon that independence; a gap, as it were, is left in the counterpoint, not least because a note plus its octave or fifth is making a sound that adds nothing significant to the sound of the fundamental tone. It becomes like a picture where the painter has simply omitted to paint—a gap or bare patch appears in the music. Musicians know of the conventional device for reproducing primitive or rustic sounds, which is to introduce a bass moving in parallel fifths. The hearer's immediate reaction is to apprehend a primitive sound, to say, "That's supposed to be an old-fashioned country dance."

Example 2 follows the same principle. In this case, all three of the chords in which two parts move in fifths are discords, so the "bare patch" symptom does not appear.

Example 3 is a product of Vaughan Williams's great sympathy for primitive music. He is purposely making use of the fact that the fifth simply reinforces the fundamental. He is here writing not four parts in the counterpoint but two.

Example 4 is quite different. Every musician on first hearing that piece (it was first heard at the coronation of

Elizabeth II in 1953, and Vaughan Williams was almost eighty when he wrote it) reacted by saying, "*Listen* to the old so-and-so! Who else could have got away with that?" Although the veteran composer may have offered a sly wink as he wrote down those closing bars, what he did was exactly what he meant to do. Try harmonizing that passage—which, mind you, is part of a perfectly conventional piece of music—in any other way and you will see what you miss. The composer wanted the bare patch, the effect of fading away into silence, an effect he often exploited in larger works, notably the end of his Sixth Symphony. The simplest way to get it in a two-page piece for a large and not primarily musical occasion was to write those parallel octaves.

What does this prove about the "law" of music? That the law is perfectly sound, but that it has limitations. The law is a good tutor—young composers must be cautioned about leaving bare patches in their counterpoint where they do not intend them to be; composers must be taught to write exactly what they mean, and most of the time they will not mean bare patches. But the law was not there in the beginning (Abraham had more than one wife) and the law is not intended to be restrictive, but liberating. Indeed, the prior law, the natural law or the "law in the mind of God," is that a composer shall write what he means so that what he means will be communicated to the hearer. To that end it is wise not to write parallel fifths and octaves unless you know exactly what you are doing.

To put it another way, remember that this particular law of music was not written down as a law by any music instructor until long after it had been found to be a wise principle by working composers. Textbooks on harmony came long after the music that exemplifies their principles, just as Sinai came long after Abraham. Moreover, the law that Jesus and Paul criticized was really the confusion of the law with natural law. Natural law says, "Society must keep the peace and generate happiness." Regulations which roughly protect society against the breach of that are not ultimate. There is no gainsaying the law as Jesus interpreted it: "You shall not hate; you shall not lust; you shall speak the truth." Without that, grief and confusion run free. But to say that people are outcasts because they rub ears of wheat between their fingers on the Sabbath is a preposterous breach of proportion. Similarly, to say that Vaughan Williams' "O taste and see" is bad music because of those octaves at the end is a breach of proportion, as it would be to say that the fifths in the other examples make the music that contains them unusable because it is incorrect. Such judgments are called pedantic, and so they are.

It should be added, of course, that the whole of this law applies only to music that uses a certain language. It is common knowledge that during the second half of the nineteenth century experiments in coining a totally new musical vocabulary were initiated, with Debussy usually thought of as the prime mover. The end product of these has been a new musical language running alongside the old one, in which the whole system of grammar and syntax is different from that which evolved from primitive western music. It may have its laws, but this one does not apply; neither does it presumably apply in other musical vocabularies that have developed in other parts of the world—but those are outside the scope of this present project.

A second example comes from a point which I ventured to make in *Words, Music and the Church* about the curious symptom of musical fundamentalism. The background proposition here is that only in a certain kind of music—a kind now very familiar—does the composer write into his score indications of every effect he requires and every note he wants played. As far as notation goes, polyphonic music obviously needs an exact and authoritative score for performance and it always had one. But the baroque kind of music in which a solo instrument, a voice, or a small group was supported by a continuo accompaniment, the device of "figured bass," in which the composer wrote for the accompanist only the bass and used figures to indicate the harmony, was not only a convenient shorthand; it was also an invitation to the continuo player to improvise whatever accompaniment his ingenuity could devise that conformed to the harmonic texture of the piece. The actual notes were not written; the player was invited to supply them, and no two players would supply exactly the same notes. Similarly in virtuoso pieces the cadenza was not written out by the earlier composers; it was an invitation to the soloist to make a personal comment on, and summary of, the music which had been built up in the movement about to come to its close. It came as a slight shock to me to realize that there are many people, especially in the United States, who have not really grasped this principle, chief among whom are those who accompany congregational singing. I shall say a little more later about the propriety of treating all hymn accompaniments as if they were figured bass or continuo.

But fundamentalism of this kind—assigning plenary authority to the written word or note—also causes people to be needlessly pedantic about the correct version of music when nobody can really say what the correct version is. Consider the debates which still continue about the interpretation of plainsong. Did they sing plainsong in the middle ages with approximations to measured rhythms? Solesmes says they didn't and we mustn't; other authorities say that they did and we may. There is actually nothing in the written music to give us assurance either way. Or we may ask what is the correct version of some old carol or folk tune, like "A Virgin Unspotted." Is it the one John Stainer used, or the one Martin Shaw used? Stainer's (in *Christmas Carols New and Old*) comes from a transcription made in 1827 from a living singer. Shaw's (in the *Oxford Book of Carols*) was from a transcription made from another living singer. Was Vaughan Williams or Benjamin Britten right about "O Waly Waly"? "Either way," we should conclude, "it's a lovely tune." There is no law about it at all. What matters most is whether the song as performed makes its effect; whether it meets the consciousness of those whose worship it is assisting.

We must add here that there are forms of music which came into vogue during the later twentieth century in which the singers are actually invited to compose as they go along, being given by the original composer only general guidelines about pitch and duration. In music of the aleatoric kind, as this is generally called, the decisions concerning the final effect of the piece are shared between the composer and the performer. In a typical simple example, William Albright's

26

"Alleluia Super-Round," from *Ecumenical Praise*, sets out 23 musical phrases, which each performer sings in order at his or her own speed, performers entering in turn, until a considerable body of sound is built up. The composer prefaces the piece with six paragraphs of instructions, the general drift of which is to encourage performers to take their own line and yet sing in a neighborly way. Thus "each singer performs independently of the other singers," but "performers should use their ears so that they might contribute most effectively to the total sound." The usefulness of such a piece is limited (the only word of text is "alleluia") but undoubtedly the experience of taking part in such a piece is one of independence plus neighborliness. In principle this is very close to the freedom commended at a theological level in the New Testament. Here, then, there is not much notion of correctness and certainly none of uniformity, apart from the natural duty of the singer to contribute and to be conscious of his neighbors, not by singing exactly what anyone else sings, but by being aware of the total effect required. The elementary discovery that pentatonic music, whatever anyone sings, cannot produce discords, has inspired many composers to contrive simple pieces of this kind (the example above is not actually pentatonic but many are). Indeed, it has been found possible to devise such musical acts without the use of any kind of a printed text. One does this by announcing some simple traditional phrase like "*Gloria in excelsis Deo*," giving a pitch, indicating that the five notes of the pentatonic scale can be used in whatever octave the singer finds comfortable, and giving the congregation some kind of a push-off from the shore. (A little preliminary warm-up is usually needed to overcome shyness in the initial stages, but there is no reason why, as a congregational response to an act such as the reading of a Scripture lesson, an aleatoric *Gloria* should not become a quite normal activity in a congregation.) Aleatoric music requires, of course, an overall director—somebody has to set it off, and, even more important, indicate where it is to stop. But it is easy to see that the focus of correctness is here in a very different place from where it is when a choir is singing Bach or Zimmermann.

These three examples serve to alert the reader to the need

for caution about what correctness or law really is in music. But there is no suggestion here that antinomianism is the Christian way. Antinomianism is the error of thinking that the law does not apply to Christians, that, for example, once converted, a Christian is free to steal or commit adultery. In an aleatoric exercise such as that mentioned above, it won't do for people to sing at whatever pitch they choose, or to go on singing after the precentor's cutoff. Although there may be no establishable correct version of this or that ancient melody, it is not appropriate for each singer to decide what version he will sing. Primitive music had its rules. The law is not ultimate, but one does not thoughtlessly disregard one's tutor.

In the normal field of church music, however, it is probably fair to say that as much damage is done by too much reverence for law as by too little. On the one hand there has always been plenty of church music whose correctness cannot be questioned, but whose dullness and lack of inspiration is equally obstinate. I suppose that the dullest hymn tune to which I was ever exposed is this:

Nobody can possibly say that that is not correct; but it would take a very volatile spirit to be inspired by it.

On the other hand, we are beginning to see in our own time a contempt for law which is, I think, fairly new, and which is perhaps a thoughtless reaction against the tedious rectitude of so much earlier music. We do very often see pieces composed and published which, using the traditional vocabulary, cheerfully ignore the "fifths and octaves" convention; and the thoughtlessness with which they do it argues a barbarous contempt for the decencies of musical conversation. For this I can see no excuse whatever. It is indecent to say that because Vaughan Williams did it we can all do it. Unless we have his insight and creativeness, and unless we seek the effect he was after, we have no right to claim him as an authority for our carelessness. (It will not be a popular view, but I hold it, that there is such a thing as a musician who is a better musician than most. Democracy of this trivial kind will get us nowhere.)

One also notices, in the work of some contemporary composers, especially in the United States, a tendency to begin in one key and end in another, not infrequently in the key a tone higher. In classical music, whose vocabulary modern musicians make use of because it is the vocabulary that communicates most easily to a nonmusical community, one of the decencies of conversation is the key-center. In all classical literature this is assumed, and its discipline produces the tonal tensions which give thrust to the musical argument of the movement. You will find in all that literature only one example, I think, of a piece beginning in one key and ending in another, Frederic Chopin's Second Ballade. There is also Franz Schubert's Second Impromptu, which ends in the tonic minor, but there the foreign key is a related key. However, a choral piece which begins in F and ends in G is not even using a related key but a device made familiar by pop music, where invention is normally so tenuous that the only way to introduce new interest is to hitch the key up a tone. I have heard organists do this with the final stanzas of hymns, blissfully ignorant that the source of their inspiration is cafeteria-Muzak. Music's argument should be more courteous and more decisive than that.

What it all adds up to is this very obvious proposition: contempt for the law is contemptible, but reverence for the law will interpret it as a living force. Jesus did not commend stealing and adultery. He commended a creative use of the law against these things, which would produce a society where positive love was constantly generated.

5

Beauty

Certain phases in the controversy between the church and the artists are perplexing and astonishing to those who overhear it from outside both worlds. While at some periods the church has been a munificent patron of art, at others it seems to have carried the restraint of art to the point of a positive cult of the ugly. In this special field of music we have the whole matter in a perspective which does not apply to the other arts, since music is, among the arts, a late developer, and those periods which witnessed the church's most generous patronage of art were those in which music was still in its infancy. In a general way, we may recall what seems to be the malignant hideousness of so much nonconformist architecture in England, and the whole puritan suspicion of visual aids to worship which has conditioned so much of modern English church life. We may recall the remarkable fact that a certain kind of zeal for souls is accompanied by what sensitive people regard as a debased taste in music and ecclesiastical decor. And with all that, we must face the persistent generosity with which the church has for many generations now offered hospitality to the second-rate. We recall Percy Dearmer's famous attack on the commercial and spiritual second-rateness which he saw in the church of his day (about 1900) in the introduction to *The Parson's Handbook*:

> A modern preacher often stands in a sweated pulpit, wearing a sweated surplice over a cassock that was not produced under fair conditions, and holding a sweated book in one hand, with the other he points to the machine-made cross at the jerry-built altar, and appeals to the sacred principles of mutual sacrifice and love.[1]

[1]Percy Dearmer, *The Parson's Handbook* (Oxford, England: Oxford University Press), introduction to the seventh edition.

There at once is a clue to the moral implications of ugliness, expressed in the phrases and thought forms of an age now past, but based nonetheless on an abiding principle. I quote it at the outset in order to arouse a sense of the complexity of the whole matter of beauty in worship.

To attack the question as near the root as we can, we must begin with the quite unquestionable if not very palatable truth that "beauty" is not a New Testament word. The word beauty appears nowhere in the King James Version; neither, in the Greek, does *kallos* or *euprepeia* or any word that can mean beauty appear in any sense but the strictly moral. Indeed, beauty in the postromantic sense is a totally unbiblical word. In the King James Version of the Old Testament, beauty translates no fewer than nine Hebrew roots; but in every case the meaning is limited to a quality and is never allowed to move over into an abstraction. Beauty is not a thing any Hebrew could have found himself seeking as an end in itself, even though it is a quality which, along with other qualities, he was prepared to ascribe to such objects as deserved it. The most famous of biblical texts on beauty, beloved of preachers at choir festivals, "O worship the Lord in the beauty of holiness" (Psalms 29 and 96), means no more than "Worship the Lord with decent ornaments" or ". . . in holy vestments"—something (as one might expect, knowing the vital concreteness of the Hebrew tongue) a good deal less abstract and romantic than what we usually take that text to mean. While the New Testament talks of charity and of truth, it does not talk of beauty. Therefore the biblical theologian will not want to use language suggesting that beauty is an autonomous or absolute category.

We can summon help at this point from St. Thomas Aquinas, who says that the beautiful is that of which the apprehension itself is pleasing (*cuius ipsa apprehensio placet*)[2] or, elsewhere, that which being contemplated pleases (*quod visum placet*). That is a definition of the beautiful, not a description of the mechanics of contemplating the beautiful, and it will not stand weight for which it was not constructed. But it bears this important comment, that for St. Thomas,

[2]Thomas Aquinas, *Summa Theologica* Ia IIae xxvii I.

31

the beautiful is neither something wholly objective, nor something wholly subjective. It is not something existing in its own right, to be sought in its own right; nor is it something having its existence wholly in the eye of the beholder, and therefore about which no general proposition can be made. Being contemplated, it pleases. It exists enough to please, but not enough to please without being contemplated.

And whom does it please? The definition is not designed to answer that. But the short answer is that it pleases a sinner. Nothing could be more obvious, and yet rarely is the consequence of this platitude taken into account. It brings us, however, to our second main proposition, which is this: that there is no hideous conventicle, no ghastly religious painting, no miserable hymn or demoralizing hymn tune, no mawkish anthem or organ voluntary, no spiritually depressing piece of church furniture, but somebody has thought it beautiful. Beautiful, I insist, not merely serviceable. All these things are adornments of worship, or are supposed to be. Nobody will call a building ugly that somebody before did not call beautiful.

Pause on this. It is the puritan strain in English religious life that has been most often accused of cultivating the ugly. But such a generalization needs careful qualification. What is really offensive about the ugliest manifestations of post-puritan church architecture is their pretentiousness. The pretentiousness implies that behind the facade there is an insufficient backing of truth and honor. In practice, it combines a large and impressive size with cheap materials, and with an implied contempt for craftsmanship. There are very few puritan meeting houses of the first generation left now, but those that do remain are not at all to be described as ugly. What they are is modest—dull, perhaps, uninspired, but never ugly in the pretentious sense. They avoid pretension as easily as they avoid the rhetorical impressiveness of a medieval cathedral, simply because their builders had no theological use for either. But when you come to a building that is really appalling, you must admit that it was deliberately made so, and that it was beautiful to its designer. If he did not call it beautiful, he would have used some other word like "fine" or "impressive," meaning that it was more than merely useful—that it not only *did* something but also *said* something.

In church music a tendency to pretentiousness first becomes noticeable after the Restoration (perhaps Purcell's Te Deum in D is the earliest example) and obtrudes itself more offensively as we move nearer the year 1900. Something disastrous happened to the aesthetics of post-reformed Christians to permit this. We here merely note that without any doubt it did happen, and return to our warning that there is no reason why it should not continue to happen today.

But we may now state the next proposition of which church aestheticians should take note, which is that no artist who really knows what he is doing would find much intelligible content in the notion that he tries to *make* his work beautiful. Here is a picture, or a piece of music, or a cathedral, that sweeps us all into ecstasy by its sheer beauty. It is not perhaps quite fair to say that to its maker the picture presents itself as a series of blobs of paint, the music as a series of marks on paper, or the church as a heap of stones. But any artist who has mastered to any degree the very arduous business of translating his conception into communicable form will tell you that the process of *making* involves very little, if any, thought about beauty. Far from its being a part of the creative activity, attention to beauty in the thing being made is one of the major temptations the artist must set aside. For beauty, as we have seen, is associated with the transaction between the work of art and the contemplator. It is an effect which the artist hopes (perhaps prays) he will achieve. But if he seeks beauty for itself, attempts to "make beautiful" his piece of music or picture, he will probably disfigure it. While he is making, it will seem to be not a beautiful thing growing under his hand, but rather, more often than not, a recalcitrant thing taking all his effort to keep it on its designed track. Thus to express what happens in the process of making is probably to attribute to the thing being made a kind of conscious will it does not have. It is really a way of saying that the artist is himself torn two ways as he makes—between the necessity of *right* making and the temptation to attend to the effect of the thing made.

This is not the place to take very far these thoughts about aesthetics in general. But it is within the terms of our brief to say that although the artist has a right, as it were, to the satisfaction that making a thing others accept as beautiful gives him, this of all rights he must not snatch at. He must resolutely and ascetically set all thoughts of it aside. When Dorothy Sayers, in her illuminating book *The Mind of the Maker*, described certain perversions of artistic techniques as illustrating perversions of the doctrine of the Trinity, she was illustrating our present point about "spirit-centered" art, art which attends too much to its effect on the contemplator. In the sphere of music I think that the composer in the romantic period whose work shows most conspicuously the signs of structural distortion because of insufficient resistance to this special temptation is Sergei Rachmaninoff. Two eminent examples of distortion in the work of this composer, who at his best was a craftsman of great excellence, are the structure of the last movement of his Third Piano Concerto, which is thrown completely out of proportion by the enormous and fantastic episode in E flat, supported almost throughout on a tonic pedal, lasting from sections 48 to 58; and the *Lento* section of the E Minor Prelude for Pianoforte, op. 32, no. 8, where everything is held up for a long inverted pedal on B which introduces ravishing sounds without advancing the argument an inch. The first example is the more disastrous from the structural point of view, in that its foreground material is taken from a subject that has already been used extensively in the first movement of the same work; a failure of idea has quite certainly been the occasion of the composer's taking refuge in beauty-hunting.

It is a consciousness of the elusiveness of beauty and of the dangers of hunting it that makes aestheticians write as J. E. Barton does in *Purpose and Admiration*, where he admirably says that "discussions about sublimity are the very worst beginning for an orderly appreciation of art." A little later he writes that the maker of a poker is as much entitled to artistic asceticisms as the painter of a picture:

> Hegel once said that "an old woman likes a sermon full of texts she knows, so that she can nod her head wisely when she hears them." This might be a parable of our commonest

attitude to the art of the painter. It is an attitude which ignores largely, if not wholly, the principles we ought to have learned from the art of the pokermaker. It ignores the cardinal fact that a good painter, like a good pokermaker, sets out to give us something new, something he had made himself, and something which has for us the double value of perfection and freshness.[3]

It is interesting to compare this with another statement by St. Thomas about beauty, upon which Maritain comments in his *Art and Scholasticism*: "For beauty three things are required: in the first place, integrity or perfection (*integritas sive perfectio*), for whatever is imperfect is *eo ipso* ugly; in the second, proportion or harmony (*proportio sive consonantia*); in the third, clarity (*claritas*); for there is a splendor in all objects that are called beautiful."[4]

It is design that is paramount in the scholastics; you will get your *nitor* (here rendered "splendor") if you attend with care to *proportio sive consonantia*; and attending to them will take all your time. Maritain compares Augustine's *splendor ordinis* and *unitas formae pulchritudinis*.[5] Wherever you touch the medievals you find them healthily free of any kind of false sublimity in their discussions of beauty.

We may observe in passing, and shall later have to consider in greater detail, that Mr. Barton's "newness" is a very large part of that area in the artist's work which falls under what we have already called the gospel principle. We shall find that one of the important questions to ask about a piece of music, even about a piece of church music, is "What in this is new?" Our judgment will have to be on the gospel plane, not on the legal plane.

But for the moment we must follow where our present argument is clearly leading. What is this preoccupation with sublimity that bedevils our thinking about art, and about music, and about church music? The popular name given to it is romanticism, and we will now turn to an investigation of what that means.

[3]J. E. Barton, *Purpose and Admiration* (Christophers, 1932), pp. 252, 253.

[4]Maritain, *Art and Scholasticism* (Sheed and Ward, 1939), pp. 24ff., 159.

[5]Augustine, *De Vera Religione* 4, cited by Maritain, *Art and Scholasticism* (Sheed and Ward, 1939).

6

Romanticism

"Romantic" is, among reforming church musicians, a primary adjective of opprobrium. If you want to hear the word pronounced with the highest content of venom, you should hear it from the lips of a modern reformed pastor in Switzerland, speaking German. In stating just what we mean by romanticism and discussing the theological answer to its defects, it is instructive to recall what Professor C. S. Lewis wrote some years ago on this subject.[1] He categorized romanticism in literature in seven forms: (1) the dangerous or adventurous; (2) the marvelous; (3) the titanic and larger-than-life; (4) the abnormal or anti-natural; (5) the egoistic, inward-looking, or subjective; (6) the rebellious with respect to civilization and convention; and (7) the sensitive to natural objects, associated with "solemnity and enthusiasm." William Blake's famous poem beginning "And did those feet in ancient time...." embodies most of the traits of romanticism in letters. Our modern use of them with a splashy tune by a fine English composer is a capital example of romanticism in practice. Lewis goes on to speak of romantic experience in terms of (8) an intense longing which is *in itself* prized as an object whose attainability is impossible and (9) a sense of mystery in the thing longed for.

Lewis was an acknowledged master of English studies and a very able Christian apologist and moralist, but he was not a biblical theologian. I do not think that he intended, in his categorization of romanticism, to give us clues to the understanding of Old Testament religion. However, it is impossible not to be struck by his precision in listing the spectrum of natural human needs to which romanticism provides an illusory answer and the religion of the Bible a real answer.

We can summarize the Christian answer to romanticism

---

[1]C. S. Lewis, *Pilgrim's Regress* (Bles, 1943), preface to the second edition.

in a sentence: Christian doctrine substitutes eschatology for romanticism. The argument which leads us to this conclusion takes us again into the Old Testament.

Eschatology in place of romanticism is what really disposes of categories 8 and 9 in the series above, where romanticism has a great longing for a distant object which is more real than the object itself, Christian doctrine introduces the whole category of hope. The longing is not rejected but fully admitted. It is often expressed as a personal longing for heaven, and thus it appears in many famous hymns, like those taken from the last pages of the *Hora novissima*.[2] It is also expressed in the "groaning and travailing" of Rom. 8:22. But the object longed for, though mysterious, is to Christians the most real thing of all: the personal enjoyment of the beatific vision, or the consummation of the Kingdom (Rev. 11:15). So real is it to the Christian consciousness that the book of Revelation is constantly under fire from those who find it too concrete and particularized in its symbolic pictures of the heavenly city.

The whole Christian system of the New Testament is prepared by the developing religious consciousness of Israel recorded in the Old. Here we hear again and again the deep notes to which romanticism without a Christian system was trying to find an answering chime.

Professor Lewis's first category was that of adventure and danger. This is exactly how the early Israelites were taught to look at life, through the archetypal allegory of the Exodus. A certain kind of security was forbidden to them. The technique was worked out, with much pain and grief, in the great trek of the Exodus. When Nehemiah reminded a later generation that the benefits of a settled civilization might poison the roots of their religion, he ordered that the sense of pilgrimage by symbolically revived in the Feast of Tabernacles (Nehemiah 8). Man's capacity, indeed his need, for wonder (category 2) is adequately covered by the august sense of God which was native to Israel from the earliest times and which is archetypally symbolized in Sinai. The sense of the titanic and the sense of the abnormal (3 and 4)

[2] EH Numbers 371, 392, 412 and 495. The most celebrated English hymn taken from this is "Jerusalem the Golden."

are answered in primitive religion by the people's consciousness of heavenly and demonic agencies, angels and devils,
which certainly left them with little need to invent any
more. The egoism and introversion that are characteristic of
so much romantic literature (5) represent a need which is
met in the Israelites' sense of vocation. The revolt against
conventional civilization (6) is sublimated, at best, in their
sense of being in this world but not of it, and also in the
prophetic rebukes of both the foreigners' idolatries and the
Israelites' own backslidings. As for nature (7), the most
obvious and familiar of all the romantic categories, nothing
in the Old Testament is more impressive than the sensitive
insight which brought Israel, at its most perceptive, between
the Scylla of pantheism and the Charybdis of gnosticism.
Nature to them is not God, but natural objects are very
decidedly vehicles of the Word of God. Out of primitive tree
worship and hill worship they brought the insights we as-
sociate with the holy mountain, holy not in itself but because
God spoke from its height, and the great stones of commem-
oration and sanctity, like Bethel and Ebenezer, which reminded future generations of the presence of God.

The Old Testament is so nearly romantic. Indeed, it is in
one sense romantic precisely in its incompleteness. For the
heart of the Old Testament religious consciousness becomes
in the end the Messiah, the hope of the race; and never was
the romantic delusion more completely and decisively acted
out than in Israel's response when its Messiah actually came.
Here was the Messiah they had hoped and lived for; yet their
reaction at every level was, just like the romantic who finally
lays hands on the thing he has longed for: "This is very
disappointing."

All this prepared the way for Christian doctrine, which
has the answer to the needs exposed in all life and met partly
in the Old Testament. The answer is there in the finality, in
what has been called the "realized eschatology," of the
Christian revelation. Romanticism is rebuked and healed
there. Inasmuch as it loves the longing more than the
achievement, romanticism is rebuked, because the revelation is the achievement. In a sense, what the spirit of
adventure and the spirit of wonder are yearning for is

achieved, and they have no more to long for. It is found in the end to be sin to love the longing more than the thing. This is Israel's sin. It is sin to reject Revelation if we love thinking about angels and devils, imagining and inventing them, more than we love making friends with the angels and fighting the devils to whom a name and local habitation have now finally been given. It is sin to love egoism more than the courage and new being that defensive egoism always aims to achieve. Nature is redeemed through the sacramental principle, and "all things are yours; for you are Christ's; and Christ is God's" (1 Cor. 3:22-23).

Why then did romanticism, as Professor Lewis expounds it, come into action at all? For the simplest and most obvious of reasons—that an age without a Christian anchor followed an age in which these old, pre-Greek, pre-metaphysical Christian categories were accepted by those ordinary people from whom our artistic stock sprang. Romanticism is an anarchic and disobedient consequence of faithlessness. One could almost call it an anarchic and disobedient reversal of medieval *romance*. Looking at history to see from which countries the romantic movement sprang makes this evident. What, after all, is Blake, one of the authors of romanticism, but a one-man religion, a self-generated religious and philosophic system, full of that longing, rebellion, sensitiveness to human need, and affirmation of human *being* which any educated man ought to have, and for which the religion of the Bible provides at every point?

We must now attend to the very important fact that romanticism in music, and therefore by derivation romanticism in church music, is in itself a peculiar phenomenon. Once again we have to remember that music is, among the arts, a late developer. The consequences of this are of great importance, and if we neglect them our judgment of what the church has done with music will go astray. Painting, architecture, letters, and sculpture had all come to maturity by the Reformation. What was the church of post-Christian society to do with these arts—arts fully matured, arts which had been usefully employed by the church in other ages?

The situation with music was different, in that the maturity of the art came virtually within the post-Christian period.

There is an enormous ambiguity—a heaven-sent ambiguity—about the place in history of J. S. Bach, to whom we shall later pay special attention. The general view is that all music of maturity, being inextricably mixed up with the romantic rebellion, is useless to the church, and that the church's place of repentance must be historically prior to the achievement of that maturity. Hence, I suppose, comes the commonly heard view that church music must, to save its soul, go back to plainsong, or go back to the Tudors. The assumption is that church music "fell" in a way comparable to the fall of Adam, sometime in the eighteenth century, somewhere between Bach and Beethoven (or, as Karl Barth would no doubt hold, between Mozart and Beethoven). Assumptions of this kind we must here impugn. Altogether too much is made, for example, of the difference between Chopin as a romantic and Bach as a classic. It matters enormously, however, that we fully understand what is at the heart of romanticism, and how the contemporary case against it should be prepared.

7

Romantic Church Music

However much we may wish to criticize the romantic idiom in church music, however clamorous our desire to distinguish what is theologically safe from what is perilous, we have to begin from the fact that in Great Britain and America an enormous proportion of the music actually used in church is romantic. There is plenty of church music that is pre-romantic and post-romantic, but in the parishes and dissenting churches, and in the Roman Catholic Church most of all, the romantic idiom is the *lingua franca* of the congregation. The highest proportion of non-romantic music is heard in cathedrals, which nowadays give a good run to the primitives and the classics, and in circles where music is performed at a high level of skill, where modern musicians, who still sound cacophonous and forbidding in the ears of congregations, get the best attention.

What we mean by the romantic idiom can be expressed in historical terms by calling it music in the language coined by Ludwig van Beethoven. But since most church music is a long way from Beethoven (he will turn in his grave if we do not insist on that), we must be a little subtler if we are to find our way through a rather intractable jungle. C. S. Lewis continues to help us if we will use him. If we set out his categories again in subclassifications we see the beginning of a track we can follow:

A. The dangerous or adventurous
   The marvellous
   The titanic
   The supernatural

B. The eogistic
   The rebellious
   The sensitive to nature

C. Intense longing
   Mystery in the thing longed for

I think that we have sufficiently dealt with category C in Chapter 6. Categories A and B settle down quite comfortably into slots in our musical experience. For romantic music, according to accepted usage, is music which preeminently deals in large ideas or music to which one would apply the adjective "expressive." It is a meeting place of the titanic and the intimate, the universal and the subjective. As such it is, at its best, a natural development from classical music; it is not in itself bad or to be written off theologically. I personally resist the tendency to write it off, or even to say that it may be appropriate for the concert hall or theater but is inappropriate in church. The only difficulty with romantic music is that it is dangerous. It demands that the composer (and the performer) keep many more balls in the air without dropping them than primitive and classical music demand. It is not incapable of being adapted to small musical forms, as the preludes of Chopin or the songs of Schubert attest; nor, as I hope to show, it is incapable of suffering the special disciplines which church music is bound to impose. But both in small forms and in church music it can show the same discomfort, and lead the composer and performer into the same snares, as one finds it doing in the large forms of opera and symphony.

One way of demonstrating simply the difference between the primitive and classical traditions on the one hand and the romantic on the other is to compare the *Passion Chorale* with J. B. Dykes's tune to "Eternal Father, strong to save." Dismiss for a moment the sense of incongruity this suggestion evokes—it is mostly the product of musical snobbery anyhow. The point here is this. The *Passion Chorale* is not a passion chorale at all, but a hymn tune derived from a secular song that J. S. Bach thought equally appropriate to Christmas and Good Friday and which Paul Gerhardt used for a hymn about God's providence (see p. 56). Dyke's tunes *Melita* was written for the famous words about seafarers and their dangers, and was written to *express* those words. It did so in the sound made by the basses and tenors in the second bar, by the use of chromatic harmony and the melodic zigzag in line three, and in the creeping chromatic melody in line five, expressing the idea of struggling against an angry sea. We are here comparing a primitive tune written in 1601 with a romantic one written in 1861. See at once how Bach stands reconcilingly in the middle. For Bach knew how to express emotional states through conventional musical symbols, and the most usual of these were chromaticism and halting melody. But whereas what we call the *Passion Chorale* was not designed to express any particular set of words, or thought indivorceable from words of any particular emotional color, Dykes's tune was designed to express words and the emotions in them. Dykes's tune expresses; the old tune merely carries. You can make this test by comparing any well-known tune of the sixteenth or seventeenth century with any tune by Dykes, and the answer always comes out the same. The bridge between the two styles is Bach himself, who has his musical symbols for evoking or observing emotion. Romanticism also has its musical symbols, but they are far more varied and subtle and therefore far more vulnerable to misuse by composers who cannot handle such powerful material.

Now for a more extreme example of classical music's shyness in expressing what we should take to be obvious emotional assents, consider Giovanni Pergolesi's *Stabat Mater*. Pergolesi was a younger contemporary of Bach—his short life (1710–36) falls wholly within Bach's lifetime—but his style is strictly Italian, and the result is that an ear tuned to the romantic wavelength finds some movements in the *Stabat Mater* intolerably flippant. Pergolesi writes to the convention of the suite—musical movements in contrasted styles. The poem he is setting may be a unity, and a unity of scarcely bearable pathos, but the canons of music demand an allegro, so an allegro is what he writes. Now this is quite different from the weird incongruities of Gioacchino Rossini's setting of the same words; for in his *Stabat Mater* Rossini tries to graft a romantic style on to a classical stem. He had been an operatic composer in his youth, and in later years produced this strange piece of sacred music without abandoning any of the operatic conventions. He sets *Cuius*

animam gementem contristantem et dolentem to this astounding
tune:

Cu - ius___ a - ni - mam ge - men - tem,___

con - tris - tan - tem___ et - do - len - tem.

without a twinge of aesthetic conscience, because his classical tradition says that this is what the music must do, let the
words say what they will. It sounds odd because his idiom is
romantic, exceedingly emotive and expressive. The trouble,
for the romantically trained ear, is that the emotion of the
music is quite different from the sense of the words. These
assumptions are nowadays being questioned, which may
account for the modest revival that this peculiar work has
recently enjoyed.

Now compare Pergolesi's *Stabat Mater* not with Rossini's,
but with Stainer's *Crucifixion*. In that work the emotions
romanticism deems appropriate to passiontide are celebrated
in music very precisely adapted to them. Nature and the subjective in the words are served as they are not served in the
classical style. There is nothing incongruous here in the way
that *Eia Mater* is incongruous in the Pergolesi. The abysmal
incongruity of Stainer's work comes from his astonishing in-
sensitiveness to bathos (the chief snare in romantic music and
letters); indeed, one might irreverently judge that his native
sensitiveness may have been bashed out of him by the shame-
less and brutal sentimentality of the libretto he chose. The
subjective element in romantic music is plain for all to see as
soon as the composers learn the language.

The marvelous, mysterious, or larger-than-life element in
romantic church music is peculiarly adapted to the spacious
context of the cathedral or large collegiate church, or for
such an occasion as a coronation; and some of the best
romantic church music, in terms of music, is on the grand
scale. It comes into its own with Parry's "I was glad," written
indeed for a coronation, and with the large conceptions of
Charles Wood, whose "O thou, the central orb" I have

44

referred to as "the authentic English cathedral sound." The cathedral service settings of Herbert Howells are a very gracious late flowering of romanticism, with their remarkable sense of awe and mystery and their combination of intimacy with majesty. Their opening subjects are always wistful—melodies very often gathered around a rising minor third—yet the architecture of the music corresponds sensitively with the architecture not only of cathedrals in general but also of the particular building to which each is dedicated. There is far more good romantic church music from the twentieth century than from the nineteenth, and this is because at the turn of the century English music began to recover its nerve and English composers developed, late in the day, the capacity to write music whose construction would stand the stress of romantic ideas. Pioneers in this were Parry (who was not primarily a church musician) and Stanford (whose church contribution was considerable). Edward Elgar showed that an English musician could "think large." Vaughan Williams, though in subject matter a reactionary against romanticism, remained in his manner and diction much more of a romantic than he is considered to be, for he was very skillful in the large forms, very much given to a rustic form of the Elgarian *nobilmente*, and always tending to think of the spacious occasion rather than the humdrum parish occasion. (Look at the tempo marks in the *English Hymnal* for confirmation of this.)

No, romantic music cannot be written off. More music is romantic than the anti-romantics allow. But what are the dangers of which we speak?

First, it is the special property of romantic music that it prejudges the audience's reaction. It assumes an audience, of course, which classical music is much less committed to assuming. Given the audience, the delicate and complex vocabulary of romanticism prescribes the reaction. Where the words are reflective the music will necessarily be of one kind, where they are jubilant, of another. A romantic does not write jubilant music in anything but a major key, and preferably one of the home keys. In the sixteenth century jubilant music could be in the Dorian mode. Romantic organ music needs a wide variety of volume levels; classical organ

45

music needs more urgently a variety of tone colors at the same volume level. The reaction today against romanticism is a questioning of the composer's right or duty to prescribe emotional responses. (See Chapter 8 of my book *Twentieth Century Church Music* for a discussion in this context.) If you have any suspicion of rhetoric or brain-washing, you will see a danger in romantic music. This attitude is natural in an age like ours which has learned to look cautiously on mass movements and manipulation of human emotions on a large scale.

In other words, romantic music is dangerous when it is sentimental. Unless the word sentimental is used in a neutral sense, what we mean by it is the manipulation of sentiment, the arousing of emotions without a corresponding excietment of reason. The case against this kind of sentimentality is simply that Adolf Hitler was a very sentimental man and Nazism a highly sentimental cult. Stand Hitler up against Lewis's scale of romantic values and the bell rings every time. Dangerous or adventurous; marvelous or wonder-working; titanic or larger-than-life; egoistic and subjective (truth is what I make it); rebellious (1933 was a revolution); sensitive to nature ("Blood and Soil")—there could hardly be a better sketch of Hitler and his creed. Sentimentality carries the overtones of both anarchy and cruelty.

> From all the easy speeches
> that comfort cruel men—

Chesterton caught the point exactly in those lines (the only ones in all hymnody which mention the subject).

Second, of the danger of the majestic and titanic, this can be said. Traditional cathedral music is magnificent in its way, but why are we so sure that cathedrals are designed simply to evoke a sense of awe and mystery? There is a good deal in our popular notion of the cathedral, or of the lovely old parish church, that is strictly nineteenth century. Professor J. G. Davies in his book *The Secular Use of Church Buildings* reminds us that the notion of the "hallowed spot" in which only church worship can be carried on is certainly not medieval and is in fact quite recent. This explains why so

46

many parish churches have, or until recently had, no church hall and sometimes not even a vestry. Whatever was done for church purposes was done in the church building. The size of a cathedral was planned not for the effect of mystery produced by music made or words said in one corner of a vast empty space, but rather for the specific and sensible purpose of providing shelter for a large number of people doing many different things. This is pertinent here, because it warns us that our notion of cathedral music is itself touched by the romanticism we attribute to cathedral music as a consequence of the cathedral's purpose. It is not a consequence; it is a parallel development of thought. Cathedrals *become* hushed and mysterious and majestic in the public mind for the same reason that music and the other arts become hushed and mysterious and emphatic.

It is only speculation, but I venture the opinion that the immense popularity of the Service of Nine Lessons and Carols at King's College Chapel, Cambridge, (when compared with the popularity of sung evensong anywhere) arose from the fact that the invention of this service aroused a response through its paradoxical quality. Here was a cathedral foundation singing not Stanford in C or Wood in the Phrygian mode but the earthy, secular, cheerful, friendly songs of Christmas. The collision of this earthiness and familiarity with cathedral remoteness and beauty caused a minor explosion in the affections of the British public. It is interesting to observe how, with the gradual rising of the standard of that choir to something as near perfection in its own line as mortals dare approach, there has been, over the fifty years of its acceptance as a national institution, a gradual de-sacralizing of the music. One by one the vestiges of cathedral romanticism have been pared away—Walford Davies's "O little town," for example, gave place to a Bach recitative and chorale, and this in turn gave place to the austere medieval hymn "*Corde natus.*" Carols of the F-sharp major Pettman school have gradually made way for the fresh simplicity of Berkeley's "I sing of a maiden," the good-humored asperities of Mathias' "Nowell," and the gaunt medieval coolness of "There is no rose." King's College Chapel will remain romantic as long as it stands; even

Thomas Tallis will sound romantic there as long as people think of the place with the affection they show at present.

The third point must, however, be a somewhat minatory statement. Romanticism does deal in the remote, the august, and the intimate; but its most fatal error occurs when it slides over into delusion. A scientific age has noticed this, but the special virtues of the scientific age (accepting evidence and suspecting intuitions) are not looked on by church people with a friendly eye. There is no doubt that the church has suffered, both in its administration and in its witness, from the error of delusion—delusion of grandeur and delusion of nostalgia. It could probably be shown that the church communities most given to the performance and approval of pretentious music are those which find the greatest difficulty in coming to terms with the harsh demands of our present age. And when romanticism turns sour the result is pretentiousness—the music of delusion. How many congregations feel it necessary to perform the Service of Nine Lessons and Carols in circumstances in which it simply cannot be effectively performed? Having performed it they are bound to feel that they did right. They are pretending to be King's of Cambridge; they delude themselves into thinking that because King's has its magical effect, the same music performed elsewhere must have it. How many places with anachronistic and ineffective choirs try to perform anthems which are not only beyond the singers' capacity but also inappropriate both to their liturgy and to their buildings? They are pretending to be cathedrals. Music can be the instrument or the cause of delusions of grandeur, and these are contrary to the Gospels.

In the same way music, especially romantic music because it is the music of the very recent past, can induce a pleasant delusion of nostalgia. It can throw the community back into a past which it (wrongly) feels was more comfortable and less demanding than the present. It is always easier to love the brother you haven't seen (or who is dead) than the brother you can see and who makes demands. This is a poisonous attitude in a church or anywhere else. Perhaps the most dangerous thing about an addiction to romantic music is its power to lock people up in a legendary past; romantic music does this the more effectively because its contact is so immediate and its appeal so amiable. But by an accident of its nature it also does something else, for the best romantic music, except in the hands of very great composers (who happen not to have written much for the church), is music in the grand style demanding large forces. Most romantic music in the smaller styles is trivial and, in the sense we discussed just now, sentimental. It evokes passion without responsibility or intellectual integrity. Therefore, unless a church is very lucky indeed the romantic addiction will ensure that its people hear a great deal of bad music, and a third delusion, that of indifferentism which accepts and honors mediocrity, will be forced on it.

If romantic music has to avoid all these hazards—the delusions of grandeur, nostalgia, and indifferentism—life is a great deal more dangerous than it looked. Supposing that, for good or for ill, most of what a choir and congregation sing has to be romantic in texture and diction, the only way they can guard against the worst dangers of romanticism is to cultivate an almost scientific precision in their choice of music. If any music is clearly pretentious and second-rate, they must rigorously exclude it no matter what protests that course may evoke.

But if there really is no self-deception—if you are *not* singing badly and pretending to sing well, or singing what is incongruous and pretending that it is congruous, or trying in any way to be a size or a quality that you know you are not, then it remains true that there is nothing inherently sinful or anti-Christian in romanticism.

8

J. S. Bach

The Archetypal Bach

The literature on Johann Sebastian Bach is, as everybody knows, copious and erudite. This brief chapter seeks to make three special points about him which bear on our argument: (1) The influences Bach assimilated and humbly allowed to work on him are absolutely different from the influences he exerted on those who came after him. This makes him a pivotal and unique figure in musical history. (2) Bach uniquely combines medieval craftsmanship with a mastery of modern musical rhetoric. (3) Bach has, with astounding results, suffered a romantic revival from which we are now being delivered in secular music but which we still allow to influence sacred contexts.

First a word on Bach's influences, prior and posterior. There is something uncannily appropriate in the historical position Johann Sebastian occupies. His life (1685–1750) stands astride the period when all that is characteristically modern began to come to life. His life was almost half over when Louis XIV died. In the remarkable family of musical Bachs covering the years 1520 to 1809 he stands almost exactly in the middle. All this is pleasantly symmetrical; but behind it is a series of important musical facts.

Ernest Newman wrote:

Bach is the supreme exemplification of the thesis that the greatest artists do not so much originate as fulfill; the supreme confutation of the notion that an artist's greatness reveals itself in the extent to which he "expresses the spirit of his age." He was neither at the head nor in the ranks of any contemporary "movement"; he originated no new form; he was almost as completely without influence on the half-century that followed his death as if he had never been born.

On the other hand, a little later, he writes:

> He was the only composer in his own day, before him, or after
> him, who was able to use to the full, in practice, the theoreti-
> cal possibilities of his art.[1]

That sufficiently places him. The vocabulary was all there, waiting to be used; the vocabulary of pure polyphony not yet to be set aside as antiquated, the vocabulary of monody now sufficiently developed to carry something weightier than light opera. Bach becomes therefore a contrapuntist worthy to stand beside Thomas Tallis and Giovanni Palestrina, and a writer of melody to whom Franz Schubert had nothing to teach.

The lack of influence to which Newman referred rests on the fact that in his own lifetime nobody knew about Bach apart from the courts and congregations where he worked. During the half-century that followed his death we gather that Mozart accidentally discovered a few of his pieces, and that Beethoven, in 1810, unsuccessfully applied to Breitkopf for a copy of the *Crucifixus* of the B Minor Mass because he thought its ostinato bass would provide a good exercise for one of his noble pupils. The *St. Matthew Passion* was revived by Felix Mendelssohn exactly a century (1829) after it was composed. All this is familiar enough; but it is important, as we shall see.

Another point is worth adding here. While Bach humbly admitted his complete debt to his predecessors in matters of form and vocabulary, and while his influence in those spheres on his successors is negligible, there is another sense in which Bach is archetypal for all music succeeding him down to Brahms in rhetoric and subject matter. I believe it can be shown that along certain important lines the roman-tic composers have nothing to add to Bach. They invent new forms; they exploit new tonal combinations; but until we come to the impressionists, the modern atonal geometri-cians, and the neo-medievalists, the whole school of sym-phonists and virtuosi owes everything to Bach.

[1]*International Cyclopaedia of Music and Musicians* (Dent, 1942), "Johann Sebas-tian Bach," by Ernest Newman.

Consider the fashion of writing series of preludes in every key. Characteristically, Bach wrote his two sets of preludes and fugues to demonstrate the virtues of equal tonality, and thus to lend a hand to a modern and not very popular development in musical mechanics. But after him came Chopin, Rachmaninoff, and the earlier romantic, Scriabin. To them, a series of pianoforte preludes is not a demonstration, but something more like a confession of faith. Chopin and Rachmaninoff, at all events, summarize themselves with remarkable completeness in their series. In them both men lay down the pattern of their technical vocabulary and schemes of key color. Bach does the same in his series, and he is the first to do it. Moreover, if you take a general view of Bach's "48," you find that they are, without intention and without, perhaps, any thought of conscious derivation, the archetype of all piano technique for the next 150 years. Pianists well know that a musician who can play the "48" has under his or her hands a comprehensive system of studies for any kind of music up to 1900. Passage-work, cantilena, cantabile, passionate rhetoric: Chopin, Liszt, Schumann, and Beethoven are all there in embryo. Furthermore, the counterpoint that is the basis of all Bach's work is indispensable to the structure of every romantic work fit to hear. No new language comes for a century and a half, and Bach did not invent the language anyhow. After Bach we have only new virtuosi of a specialized field, while Bach alone shows himself, in whatever form he uses, to be master of the whole field.

A typical device of romantic music is the use of key to provide color. We know what we mean in musical circles when referring to Beethoven's C minor, Chopin's D-flat, Brahms's B major, Berlioz's C major and so on. There is no comparable way of talking about Sweelinck's F major or Pergolesi's E-flat. We can only be sure that the baroque use of F minor to express pathos derived from the physical fact that on stringed instruments F minor can give a vibrato on every melodic note and is, at the same time, the remotest key-center to which it was safe to go in the days of unequal temperament tuning. But in Bach one begins to see possible relations between the choice of certain keys and the content of the music, and even possible avoidance of certain keys for unascertainable reasons. Consider what can happen with G minor: in the *Fantasia* for organ (S. 542), the Twenty-fifth Goldberg Variation, the *Sarabande* in the G Minor English Suite, and the *Agnus* in the Mass in B Minor we have a density of harmonic movement and a clash of highly charged musical statements which bind all four together. Again in E minor: in the organ prelude and fugue called the *Wedge* (S. 548), the E Minor Organ Sonata (S. 528), the *Crucifixus* in the Mass in B Minor, the opening chorus of the *St. Matthew Passion*, and the E Minor Violin-cello Duet the common factor is a massive canvas, a profound juxtaposition of musical thoughts, a large "sense of occasion," and an unexampled degree of pathos. Conversely, how rarely is his A major martial and how often is it gentle; how strangely he avoids B-flat; how oddly it turns out that some of his least profound work—one would almost say the only examples of work below his standard—comes out in A minor. Bach's interest in the possibilities of key considered absolutely and not relatively is, of course, testified to in the "48" themselves, but I do not think it is fanciful to see even here a foreshadowing of one of the most important inventions of the romantics.

This has much to do with our second proposition. Bach was in himself an extraordinary combination. He was in one way a child of his age, fitting peaceably into the prevailing fashions of court and church music. None of his music suggests that he is a rebellious social misfit, whatever his day-to-day sentiments may have been. At Arnstadt, Mühlhausen, and Leipzig he was an organist; so he wrote for the organ. At Cöthen he was a court musician, so he wrote secular music. At Weimar he was a choirmaster, and wrote for his choir, and at Leipzig he wrote for the august ceremonies of the Thomaskirche. He wrote eighteenth-century music, not affecting any antiquarianism; a modal chorale becomes an eighteenth-century chorus in his hands. He was content to do what this world required of him, and in this became perhaps the last of the medieval craftsmen. He was the most detached of all musicians from any preoccupation with what effect his music would have on any but those for

53

whom it was composed. The most unromantic and matter-of-fact of workmen, he was no great tragic figure, no frustrated, Byronic, melodramatic bohemian asking to be discovered by some Hollywood producer and made into a legend. He was an ordinary middle-class tradesman in music and an ordinary middle-class churchman—middle class because he is of the eighteenth century, but a tradesman and churchman because he was spiritually independent of ambition and lust for influence. It must be admitted that some who had to work with him or who employed him found him a difficult colleague or employee, but this was always because he protested, whenever he thought it right, against conditions of work that made it unecessarily difficult for him to be a good workman. He was as good a musical trade unionist as was S. S. Wesley in English history; but if his behavior was occasionally the behavior of protest, his music was preeminently the music of acceptance.

Bach and Pietism

One way in which he accepted peaceably the limitations of his place and time was in the matter of religion. Not only did he accept Christianity and remain in it faithfully, but he also accepted the particular brand of Christianity purveyed in the places where he lived. This was, broadly, pietism. And pietism is a precursor of religious romanticism.

Pietism has many forms. Initiated by P. J. Spener with his foundation of the *Collegium Pietatis* in 1670, and with the publication in 1675 of his *Pia Desideria*, it was a movement of evangelical revival typically consequent on the religious slump of the period of the Thirty Years' War. *Pia Desideria* called for six points of revival: intensified Bible study; fuller exercise by the laity of their spiritual priesthood; emphasis on the practical rather than the intellectual side of Christianity; manifestation of charity in religious controversy; a heightening of the devotional content of theological studies; and the reform and revival of preaching.[2] In modern terms this adds up to a fundamentalist outlook, a layman's religious move-

[2]*The Oxford Dictionary of the Christian Church*

ment, a contempt for the academic and cerebral aspects of Christian practice, a stress on interdenominationalism, a preference for prayer over instruction, and a system of conversion. It is helpful in understanding Bach's religious background to note that he was, to all intents and purposes, moving among and faithful to groups of loyal Inter-Varsity Christian Fellowship adherents; for that is exactly what, in its day, pietism was. If there was ever a limitation whose acceptance by Bach was heroic, it was surely that of the libretti he was called on to set to music in his *Passions* and the sacred cantatas. One recalls that Bach had much difficulty in getting hold of any tolerable libretto for the *St. John Passion*.[3] What he got in the end was a series of meditations which as soon as they break away from Scripture are, as everybody knows, heavily weighted on the side of natural personal grief and quite innocent of any rejoicing in the resurrection. Indeed, the pattern of his great choral works shows the effect pietism had on his work. We have the passion story set in the versions of three of the Evangelists, always on a very large scale.[4] The resurrection gets much hastier treatment. His most complete treatment of it is Cantata 4, *Christ lag in Todesbanden*, an unusually ferocious and dramatic piece of work. By comparison, both the *Easter Oratorio* and the *Ascension Oratorio* (otherwise called Cantata 2) are light-weights. An examination of William Scheide's exceedingly interesting pamphlet *Johann Sebastian Bach as a Biblical Interpreter* and especially his list of the biblical texts Bach set to music shows how strong is the pietistic influence.[5] Bach's apprehension of Scripture has no element of subtlety or of paradox. It is foreign to him and to the tradition in which he wrote to bid us "rejoice in the passion." There is no setting in his works of Heb. 12:2 and he never sees the passion as part of the story that leads to the resurrection.

It must be said, of course, that the contrast in scale between the *Passions* and the works devoted to the resurrection owes a good deal to the fact that the ceremonious

[3]Basil Smallman, *The Background of Passion Music* (SCM, 1957), pp. 13ff.

[4]The St. Mark version has disappeared and the St. Luke, sometimes attributed to him, is spurious.

[5]William Scheide, *Johann Sebastian Bach as a Biblical Interpreter* (Princeton, 1952), Princeton Pamphlets, no. 8.

reading or singing of the passion story has its origins in medieval liturgical practice. The Bach *Passions* are the apex of a structure that began with a recognition that the Gospels for Palm Sunday and Good Friday are, unlike all other eucharistic Gospel passages, immensely long, and lend themselves to dramatic treatment. Musical developments of this had already passed through many stages, from primitive plainsong reading-chants via William Byrd to certain eccentric variations on liturgical practice which Bach set aside in returning to the setting of a single Gospel story. But allowing for all this, the intimacy, the vast time scheme, the combination of loving attention to detail and massive overall conception of works taking far longer to perform than liturgy could accommodate, or indeed than any single piece of music had yet been known to take, are all the products of pietism. If pietism reserves all its expository energies for the passion, all its theological attention for the atonement, and all its sense of liturgical drama for this one occasion (in no other sense was pietism liturgically oriented), then we must ascribe to this religious culture everything distinctive about the Bach *Passions*.

But because he is essentially a craftsman, working in music without thought beyond the work, Bach's involvement with pietism made no difference whatever to the quality or texture of the actual music. We may well raise serious doubts about the sufficiency of the pietistic approach to the Christian faith, but nobody who does so can possibly claim a corresponding insufficiency in Bach's music. In William Scheide's admirable phrase, there is "no music with more solid earthbound vitality" than Bach's. The very limitations of pietism he turned to God's praise; for the repudiation of subtlety involved a repudiation of poetry, and produced inevitably a naive libretto which at least refrains from attempting anything more than a lyric virtue.

One other small matter must be noted here. Pietism, with its emphasis on congregational participation in worship, was much given to hymns. Its greatest poet is Paul Gerhardt (1607-76), whose hymns show pietism at its noblest.[6] Bach,

[6]English translations of Gerhardt include "Commit thou all that grieves thee" (H 446) and "O sacred head" (H 75).

with a characteristic blending of the new pietism and the ancient dramatic technique of bringing the audience onto the stage, familiar in the medieval mysteries, interpolates chorales in the narrative and meditation of the *Passions*. I hope to show later what an extraordinary, unexpected, and sometimes disastrous influence this technique had on later church music practice. It is one of the most mysterious paradoxes in the story of this most paradoxical of musicians. For the moment I merely recall what I amplified in my book *The Music of Christian Hymnody*, that in Bach's settings of these tunes he exemplifies all at once the heart of his musical "archetypalness." The melodies themselves are old and familiar, as familiar to his congregations as "When I survey the wondrous cross" is to English and American congregations. However, the settings are entirely in eighteenth-century style—broad, courtly, and impressive; harmony and counterpoint are substituted for unisonal irregular song style of Martin Luther's day. Nowhere do we see better than here Bach's utter refusal to be anything but a child of his own age. Here is no denial of history, no fugitive archaism. This is no place to make educational gestures toward raising their taste by insisting on original versions. I do not know whether, after a look at the chorales in the *Passions*, it is necessary to say any more about Bach's self-forgetfulness and innocence. We need not attribute these to him as costly virtues. We do not say he achieved this against the stream of what fashionable musicians were doing or what the church was demanding. The fact that Bach's *Passions* are entirely unliturgical, and therefore a break from the original form and purpose of musical passions as conceived in the days of William Byrd, is not evidence of rebelliousness, but evidence of acceptance. Pietism was unliturgical. Bach's supremacy is precisely in that quality of acceptance he exemplifies in history.

If any explicit proof is needed for the proposition that Bach's music indicates acceptance rather than romantic protest, we need only bring as evidence the curious and not always widely advertised fact that Bach is the greatest hymnologist among the great composers. It is hardly too much to say that, excepting only the Mass in B Minor, his whole output of sacred music rests on the folk song of Lutheran pietism as a building rests on its pillars and cornerstones. The drama of the *Passions* is provided by the audience participation demanded by the hymns:

"Lord, is it I?"

'Tis I, whose sin hath bound thee,
with anguish did surround thee
and nailed thee to the tree.

St. Matthew Passion, nos. 15–16

All the sacred cantatas are founded on, or use at their climatic points, Lutheran hymns; and all the genuinely sacred organ works are similarly commentaries on hymn tunes. It is impossible to judge whether the preludes and fugues for organ were designed to be sacred music, but on the whole the evidence is against it. On the other hand, it is difficult to resist the judgment that Bach's greatest organ music is found in the Eighteen Chorale Preludes (S. 651–668), the Orgelbüchlein (S. 599–644), and the Klavierübung, Part 3 (S. 669–689), all of which are devoted to chorales.

In both cantatas and chorale preludes Bach was working over ground that had been prepared, often with distinction, by his predecessors, notably Dietrich Buxtehude and Johann Pachelbel. But here as elsewhere Bach carries old form into new musical dimensions, accepting and then transforming. Uniquely among musicians, he gave the greatest honor to the most commonplace form of church music—the hymn.

Bach and the Romantics

Our third proposition is that Bach, by one of the great ironies of musical history, suffered in due time a romantic revival. This has now, thanks to the arbiters of modern musical taste, begun to pass into history. We will refer to Bach's romantic revival only briefly.

In the first place, Bach became familiar to several generations as musicians arranged his works for musical media other than those for which he wrote them. This in itself could not have offended him—Bach was himself one of the world's great arrangers. But the tendency, probably invented by Liszt and certainly carried on by his pupil, Tausig, was to arrange his works in a style more impressive and less reticent than his own. The long series of large-scale organ works arranged for concert performance on the pianoforte contains several comments on history, one of which is that works for the organ are such that one must normally go to church to hear them. They are not, however, always played when one goes there because, as in Bach's case, they are very difficult to play. But, says the listener, they are enjoyable, especially when played on a large nineteenth-century organ. Then, say the musicians, let us recapture this impressiveness, and transcribe the organ works for the pianoforte in such a manner that their difficulty is certainly not concealed from the audience and the performer's reputation will not suffer. Thus we have Tausig and Ferruccio Busoni and others giving the organ works a concert ethos that is purely romantic—a larger-than-life hero-worshiping ethos which is far from the strictly chamber music atmosphere for which they were designed. A similar romanticism can be seen in the smaller arrangements of chorale preludes and cantata movements. Dame Myra Hess some time ago arranged for piano the Adagio in A Minor from the Toccata, Adagio, and Fugue in C for organ. In her arrangement, which insists always on reproducing a 16-foot tone in the bass (and at one or two points certainly reproduces sounds Bach's harpsichord could not have made, since its extreme depth was 16-foot F), Dame Myra subtly altered the "cool" climate of the original to a "warm" climate, altered innocence to sophistication, and austerity to richness.

We may further recall orchestral arrangements of organ works which used to be popular, such as Ottorino Respighi on the *Passacaglia* and Elgar on the Fantasia and Fugue in C minor. There is also a tendency to treat Bach like Handel and to assemble choruses of enormous size and organs of vast resources for his interpretation. The conspiracy to make Bach a concert-hall draw has been now halted by the advocates of the baroque organ, the harpsichord, and the chamber orchestra and choir.

We contend simply here that this archetypal church musician was honored with the unique vocation of singlemindedness, was equipped with a fully developed musical vocabulary, and alone of all musicians since 1600 was an example of that acceptance which in more sophisticated days became a lost virtue. We also contend that delusions of grandeur and magnificence in the cause of church music are decidedly not to be fathered on Bach, but are part of the conspiracy of admiration to which he was subjected by the romantic generation.

Latter-Day Bach

It is worth noting, however, that in the 1960s the cult of Bach has undergone an important change. Following the baroque revival of the fifties, a popular reassessment of Bach has placed him about halfway between the exalted culture of the pure baroque and that which uses the harpsichord as a jazz instrument. I refer chiefly to Les Swingles, whose LPs, first of Bach's music and then of other eighteenth-century pieces (including Handel and Mozart), became best sellers, have resoundingly demythologized the music they perform. Their technique is to rearrange for vocal singing (sometimes with percussion and/or double-bass pizzicato) music of the classical sort originally written for instruments (a reversal of the Liszt-Busoni technique of arranging for a virtuoso pianist, or of the Respighi-Elgar technique of rearranging for orchestra, works written for organ or for voices). It is even more obviously a reversal of attitude; for whereas the romantic arrangers blew up the original into something more sumptuous than the composer had conceived, the new arrangers reduce it to something essentially simpler. The new style is much less a vulgar vandalism than the old, simply because the human voice is the original musical instrument, and in classical music what is written for instruments is always founded on what is singable. One remembers Sir Donald Tovey's insistence, in his commentaries and notes in the Associated Board edition of Bach's "48," that the right performance will almost always result from the player's singing a phrase before playing it.

Les Swingles catch the spirit of Bach in revocalizing his fugues and suite movements and in their swinging rhythmical treatment of the finished music. They do not, of course, set it to vocal *words*; that they are content to leave to Charles Gounod or that genius Ebenezer Prout, who found words for so many Bach fugue subjects, such as these for the G Minor Fugue in the "48" Book 2:

Oh
good morning
good morning
have you used your Pears soap today?

Les Swingles are at the same time more serious and more lighthearted than this; they anticipate, in the present argument, the protest against romantic reverence with which we shall have to deal shortly. They turn upside down the tradition of making Bach acceptable by replushing his music which Leopold Stokowski's orchestration of the Toccata and Fugue in D Minor and Myra Hess's pianizations of the chorale preludes made so popular a generation ago.

Loussier is different in that he performs a *tour de force* in controlling a number of instruments, including a piano, an electronic organ, and various percussion devices in reinterpreting Bach. With Les Swingles he made Bach dance in a manner to which Bach would not have objected; but he exploited certain strictly jazz idioms not only in his reinstrumentation, but also in linking Bach's device of quasi improvisation in florid melodic lines with the "jazz break," thus producing new improvisations which are Bach-like yet also contemporary. Musically Les Swingles scored more heavily because of the essential modesty of their aim, which is more in Bach's spirit than the strictly virtuoso aspect of Loussier's performances. But both these and entertainments such as George Malcolm's "Mr. Bach goes to Town" and the subculture of "P. D. Q. Bach" do at least make decisive gestures against romantic reverence.

That, however, is not the most important event in the strange journey Bach has made in our own lifetimes. What we refer to finally is the contemporary effort to reproduce the sounds Bach intended. Forty years ago Bach recitals were given on pianos; now they are scarcely tolerated on any instrument but the harpsichord. Even within the LP age, recordings of Bach's Brandenburgs were still influenced by a romantic and grandiose conception of what the music was about. The recent replacement of all this by recordings of Bach's work made by the *Concentus* of Vienna shows in what direction the cult of Bach has moved. Above all, the insistence by organ builders on devising organs with clarity of sound that will make Bach's counterpoint audible has produced a radical revolution in organ design.

This exposes a problem in aesthetics which the enthusiastic sometimes overlook. A great deal of what has happened since people endeavored to treat Bach as those a generation ago in Britain treated some famous pictures—by cleaning them—is clear gain. However, the field in which the gain has been made is frequently mistaken. The gain is aesthetic; that is, a much pleasanter sound is made now than was formerly. The kind of surprised delight with which we hear the *Concentus* replacing the trumpet with the recorder in Brandenburg II has in it, one admits, a touch of "So *that's* how it was meant to sound!" But the greater part of the pleasure is simply in what the ear receives. It is the same with the *Concentus* version of the great choral works; the pleasure consists not least in the modesty, the chastity, and the removal of pomp which performances on this scale celebrate.

How Bach's music was meant to sound is not as easily proved as one might at first think. To offer an elementary question, if it is true that no mechanical instrument, such as an organ or a harpsichord, was in Bach's day (or is in ours) a perfect instrument, to what extent do we do Bach a service in reproducing the imperfections of those instruments? Of course, to some extent we refuse to do this. It is probable that Bach's organ was seldom in tune; we don't de-tune modern organs to reproduce that effect. But what exactly is the philosophy behind the revival of flat parallel pedalboards, and cumbersome stop draws which are, as they often were in the eighteenth century, placed out of the player's reach? If one argues that a flat parallel pedalboard is actually more comfortable for the player and that the radiating concave kind was a mistaken invention making things more difficult, then the argument is both intelligible and decisive. But simply to insist on reproducing the conditions in which Bach worked is to make a historical gesture which may have a pedagogic use but not a musical one. A Bach organ might well have been unwieldy and had a noisy action; some of this incidental clatter, people say, is agreeable and quaint. Does the preservation of it bring music to life, or is it no more than a romantic concern with the reproduction of historical details? A fine eighteenth-century house is something we admire for its proportions, less for its plumbing.

The problem becomes more tricky when attempts are made to reproduce the sounds Bach made and heard. Aside from the high degree of guesswork involved, the question asked less often than it should be is whether the result is in any sense pleasant listening. It is right to be cautious about an insistence on this, because our ears need a sort of aesthetic disinfecting before we can appreciate new sounds. If we are used to the sound of Bach played in an English cathedral on a 1910 Willis, the sound of the same piece played in the chapel of Duke University, North Carolina (on a 1976 Flentrop with no swell boxes and very keen voicing), comes as a surprise. That sort of surprise should never be represented as something to be avoided or rejected. But let me here issue a quiet warning about confusing historical authenticity with beauty. It is not self-evident that Bach, or any other composer of that time, would have totally rejected every new development in technology, especially with respect to the organ, that took place after his time. And it is dangerous to assume that pianists who used to play Bach or organists who played him on 1910 Willis instruments were ill-educated musicians.

9

The Body

Johann Sebastian Bach was an eminent example of the literal observance of biblical commands to the musician. Much of what a musician has now come to regard as his right, he renounced. That his renunciation was made possible and even natural by his circumstances and temperament is arguable, though not self-evident. If ever a musician can be said to have lived out in his musical technique the Old Testament's implicit prohibition of self-interest and its implicit injunction to self-denial, it was he. It can also be said, on the evidence of Chapter 7, that the main weight of the case against unregenerate romanticism is its discouragement of that virtue, and at some points even its positive encouragement of the corresponding vice.

It is time to go a little deeper into doctrine. Our last chapter brought us accidentally face to face with a religious system (pietism) which has clear limitations and whose own eighteenth-century history demonstrates its special vulnerability to spiritual self-interest. We hold that J. S. Bach was able to make a virtue of its weakness. But having encountered pietism, and on the grounds that we assess it as a sectional and partial Christian system, we must now say on what positive principles we believe the church's authority vis-a-vis the musician to rest.

We must fairly admit that the church is entitled to criticize musicians who work for it, and, when needful, to control them. Church music is subject to a kind of criticism from which music outside the church is exempt. It would be ridiculous to suggest that there is one standard for the sacred and another for the secular. We do not mean this, nor do we hold that the "benefit of clergy," which seems to have exempted church music from the need to reach the standards that secular music demands, is anything but unhealthy. The opposite is nearer the mark. For while church music is not exempt from the requirements music in general must meet, it stands also under the discipline associated with its being used to further the aim of worship. It is always used in a context where the performers are not exclusively, and the hearers are not even primarily, concerned with music in itself.

It seems reasonable to assume that a musically informed church authority and a theologically informed musical authority can between them work out a counterpoint of criticism and precept in these matters. I am afraid, however, that this has very rarely happened and does not appear to be happening at all in our time. No institution devoted to the study of church music should be without a theologian in residence. There are, in the United States, several places where music and theology have been pursued on the same campus without any communication developing between the two disciplines. Whether this is because of a failure to tackle the problem or of opportunities tragically missed, the situation is not as it should be. We must look for a juxtaposition of the disciplines and dialogue between them. This could happen, for example, if a seminary were to house a church-music department where the theology and music students mingled freely with each other and the faculties were likewise in communication with one another.

Fundamental to a correct understanding of our obligations here is a clear understanding of the connection between the church, as in the expression "church music," and Christ, who is the Head of the Church. St. Paul roundly states that the connection is so close that it can be expressed in the phrase "the body of Christ." An able linguistic study of the word "body" in this phrase can be found in J. A. T. Robinson's book *The Body*. L. S. Thornton's *Common Life in the Body of Christ* presents a fuller account of this subject. Careful pondering of both studies is advised for any who would follow further the line of argument suggested in these pages.

The immediate context of the classic phrase "the body of Christ" as it appears at the end of Ephesians 1 is of the greatest importance for discovering a right doctrine of behavior and principle in all church matters. The writer of that Epistle is concerned with asserting the lordship and victory of Christ, vindicated in the resurrection.

> I do not cease to give thanks for you, remembering you in my prayers, that the God of our Lord Jesus Christ, the Father of glory, may give you a spirit of wisdom and of revelation in the knowledge of him, having the eyes of your hearts enlightened, that you may know what is the hope to which he has called you, what are the riches of his glorious inheritance in the saints, and what is the immeasurable greatness of his power in us who believe, according to the working of his great might which he accomplished in Christ when he raised him from the dead and made him sit at his right hand in the heavenly places, far above all rule and authority and power and dominion, and above every name that is named, not only in this age but also in that which is to come; and he has put all things under his feet and has made him the head over all things for the church, which is his body, the fulness of him who fills all in all (Eph. 1:16–23).

It seems to be the writer's purpose to show the fainthearted rural deanery at Ephesus that the heart of their calling is in the resurrection, that they are one with him to whom all this power was given through his resurrection. In another place he shows similarly that the church thus shares intimately in the humiliation and death of Christ through baptism (Rom. 6:1–11), and elsewhere expresses his personal hope for a share in the suffering and resurrection of his Lord (Phil. 3:10).

While Paul was writing to a local church or group of churches in doctrinal difficulty, this principle may be applied perfectly well in our corner of the field. The gift of God to the church is this union with Christ. It is therefore to be expected that in all matters of behavior the church will show the humiliation and the resurrection of Christ. Many writers have applied this in other moral fields; why should church music be dispensed from this grace?

What, on the face of it, has music to do with the suffering and victory of Christ? It has much to do with it when we remember that music cannot be made at any level without the cooperation of sinners who are redeemed by that suffering and resurrection, but whose grasp of God's gift is always partial and hesitating. Consider then the great temptation the Church always faces—to live confortably in the world, and to gain prestige, security, and worldly honor. This kind of warning note is sounded in the writings of Dietrich Bonhoeffer and Emil Brunner, and has found strident echoes in the apostles of the "new theology" of the 1960s (e.g., J. A. T. Robinson and Colin Morris). This corresponds well with the pressure brought by the world to bear on Jesus. It is there in the temptation (Luke 4:1-13), and it is there every time they wish to make him a king (e.g., John 6:15). There is always a sense in which the church must take to heart the text, "Woe to you, when all men speak well of you, for so their fathers did to the false prophets" (Luke 6:26). Both the composer and performer must exercise vigilant care against the temptation to write and perform in such a way that men "speak well"; it is this which lies behind that beauty-hunting, that craving for attractiveness, which disfigures so much of the music of the eighteenth and nineteenth centuries.

Allied with this is a temptation to exert influence of a kind not demanded by or exemplified in the Master. There is always pressure on the church to try to be greater than its Lord. Certain forms of evangelism are tainted with this defect. It means that along with an unregenerate desire for power goes an unwillingness to encounter tension or difficulty. There is a danger that in the composition and practice of church music the church will always turn to what is easy and familiar, seeking to bring men to Christ by a route which bypasses the way of the cross. Music come by in that frame of mind will not profit the people of God.

But lest any think that we are beginning to build a case for the aesthetic highbrow, to whom almost everything that appeals to the ordinary man is common and unclean, let us hasten to say that one of our Lord's major gestures against pharisaism was in the hospitality and "unshockableness" with which he received into his company all kinds of people for whom society as a whole had no use. He was much too

67

cheerful for the very religious among his enemies, and his disciples were far too sociable (Mt. 11:19, Luke 7:34). Provided we always bear in mind that the Son of Man was not in fact a glutton and a winebibber, and that the company he kept was able to benefit from his healing and fortifying presence without leaving any stain on him, these tests are a salutary reminder that pride and aloofness have no part in the church musician's ministry.

The essence of the gospel which gives life to the church lies in the complete involvement of Christ with the world, together with his moral transcendence of it. The doctrine of the church from which all criticism must proceed has in it a dynamic paradox of "no" and "yes." The church that was founded in the incarnation, passion, and resurrection of Christ is not an institution which invariably says yes to the world, nor one which invariably says no. It is as fastidious as the man seeking a goodly pearl and as hospitable as the dragnet (Mt. 13:45–47). Therefore if any music is composed or performed with an eye simply to attracting the unconverted, it is likely to fall into the same error we find in the parson who, in order to make users of bad language feel at home, uses bad language himself. Similarly, music written or performed by people who select only the most sensitive and best instructed people for disciples will be too much "on its dignity" to help anybody. There needs to be, in composition and choice, a combination of the yes and the no that corresponds as exactly as our sinful nature allows to the yes and no that are in the Word of God.

The most obvious fact to which we can point, and which needs little supporting argument, is that in the first stage of music's maturity, the sixteenth century, church music was invariably chamber music. It was music designed to be enjoyed by its performers and, in the case of church music, designed to adorn the liturgy; but it was not primarily music to be listened to by an inactive hearer. When an ordinarily appreciative listener tells me that a whole evening of Tudor madrigals is more of a discipline than an entertainment, he not only has my personal sympathy, but he is talking good history. The madrigal—secular vocal chamber music of the purest sort—was written for performers, not for listeners; or at any rate not for an indiscriminate audience of the kind for which a modern concert piece is written.

Church music of the polyphonic school is chamber music. Because of this it is delivered at once from a whole section of temptation—from all the temptation associated with rhetorical techniques. There is in this climate no temptation to undue influence. Unless some sacred impresario (such as the popes for whom Palestrina wrote so much of his music) were to provide a build-up of publicity, there would be nothing in this music of prestige value. To that extent it is innocent. True, there is that aspect of sixteenth-century polyphonic music which Cecil Forsyth, with characteristic trenchancy, called "musical bindweed," and there was in medieval music a certain tendency to levity against which ecclesiastical authorities wrote. But it is nonetheless innocent in a way later music is not innocent, and the complaints of the church, summed up in the famous encyclical of Pope John XXII (1325), are normally directed against a lack of clarity, simplicity, and decorum which makes the words carried by the music unintelligible to the listener. It is the very reverse of that overemphasis and rhetorical indulgence which later critics impugn in more highly developed music.

It is, of course, a sense of this innocence that has caused the reaction of present-day taste in favor of the Tudors. There is a cool, impersonal eloquence about the music of this period, from whatever part of Europe it comes, that is refreshing to ears too long sated with the overripe rhetoric of the Victorians.

Some of this innocence departed in England after the Restoration and on the continent with the advent of homophony two generations before. The new convention of the accompanied tune, solo prominent and accompaniment in the background, a convention which before 1600 had been limited to the balladry of strolling players, led at once toward rhetorical development. In itself this is not a "fall," not an irretrievable step of moral retrogression. It is simply the introduction into music of a new element of risk. But post-Restoration music retains one important element of innocence in that it is written, if not in an age of craftsmanship, at least in an age of hackwork, which is less edifying than craftsmanship but more edifying than the climate of artist-mysticism which followed it. The texture of eighteenth-century music in England is invariably light, and its style highly conventional. At their best the English Restoration composers are capable of highly expressive use of the new vocabulary; but in the main the dance rhythm predominates, and the conventional style provides a fairly strict pattern into which the composer must be humble enough to fit his music. There is room here for inflated bombast of a kind—for reams of really dull music. But even if here or there we find an eighteenth-century musician who could not be described as a hack, the musical ethos of that age was such as to restrain the musician from abrogating to himself too much in the way of rights of self-expression. The same ethos that caused Lord Mornington to be thought a sorry dog for walking through the public street carrying a fiddle case imposed on music a formality which at least discouraged the more irresponsible kinds of exhibitionism.

As the eighteenth century wore on, however, the crust of culture began to crack. It became very clear that the kind of music, which since the English Restoration had irrigated a church scene that puritan repressions had rendered somewhat arid, was safe only in the hands of professionals. The gap between the professional and the amateur suddenly widened. The great psalm tunes of the puritan era stood alongside the splendors of Byrd and Gibbons as a monumental amateur answer to the culture of the professionals. Once a far more flexible, expressive, and subtle kind of music was admitted to the church scene, it took a great deal more handling. The later eighteenth century produced very little professional music and a huge quantity of music associated with the evangelical revival. This music was at first produced by professionals like J. F. Lampe, but it was not long before the new music centers that grew up in the charity foundations demanded a quantity of simple music, which too quickly became vulgar and trite. This was the first phase of inflation in church music taste. It was one thing when Purcell handled explosive material to splendid purpose in a dramatic verse anthem like "They that go down to the sea in ships" about 1690; it was quite another when a half-literate composer, whose piety rather than skill recommended him, made a contribution to the *Lock Hospital* collection of hymns and anthems, or to Mr. Rippon's *Selection* a century later.

So at last we come to an age in which vulgarity becomes a serious concern. It was not explicitly a concern until the critics came along to expose it several generations later. Those who used vulgar music were quite satisfied with it. Those who would not have cared for it were not exposed to it. The church in England was not much of a "body" in those days, and indeed the very existence of such criticism of vulgar music as Vaughan Williams and Percy Dearmer made just after 1900 indicates a milieu in which people who didn't want it were likely to get it without warning. That in turn means that the Oxford Movement (1833 onward) had made the Church of England a much more cohesive body than it had been in the eighteenth century.

But, the question is, what quality is it that makes "vulgar" a pejorative epithet? That quality, in ordinary speech, is pretentiousness. More specifically, in music of the kind we are referring to here, it is a lack of balance between rhetoric and reason. Music at its most primitive is melody—just one succession of sounds. But it is not long before melody gets support, and the primitive support is percussive—a rhythmic bang, clatter, or ring produced by some instrument like a drum or gong that does not make melody. At once there are two principles, the free-ranging melody and the earthbound rhythmic beat. Critics and historians have often referred to the psychology of this when they write of the primitive music of India, for example.

Another form of this music, a little closer to present-day experience, is music in which the earthbound principle is chiefly provided by bodily movement and sounds humanly produced, in other words, dance music. Ancient traditional dance music can use a fiddle or a pipe for the melody, reinforcing it chiefly with the movements, claps, and even shouts (but not songs) produced by people moving in time to it. The music is, so to speak, kept in order by the dance whether or not there is a non-dancer providing a rhythmic thump.

Church music has already taken off on a different track.

Since the medieval church had a quite understandable suspicion of the human body as a principle of order, the controlling force in church music was the words. Plainsong is not essentially music with a rhythmic beat, however much people may in performance have assimilated it to the dance. But even so, they didn't sing plainsong on the medieval village green; ordinary lay folk did not sing it at all.

The next and final development in Tudor times was the complex succession of stages by which music became, as we say, absolute, or free-standing, depending for the support of melody not on a drum or dance but on another melodic sound. The result is music that is essentially melody and bass. Once again, church music followed its own track for a time, producing polyphony in which what was originally almost a drone became an independent melody, and in which later more voices than two were singing at once—from the four-, five-, and six-part motets of the famous Renaissance musicians to Tallis's *Spem in alium*, composed in forty real parts.

Church music was to all intents and purposes unaccompanied. (The organ accompaniment to Byrd motets would have been no more than an unobtrusive device to keep the voices in tune. Organs, especially in Britain, had little to say for themselves in those days.) Secular music was never unaccompanied, with the exception of certain folk songs that went with a culture where instruments were unavailable. Inevitably the possibilities of melody plus melodic bass had to be explored, but in the earlier examples of such music the bass is very clearly a different sort of music from the melody. It is still the rational principle controlling the ecstatic or rhetorical principle of melody. Keys settled down, and the tonic, dominant, and subdominant formed most of what the bass contributed to the piece. The earliest opera brings the new cult of the clever vocal soloist and the beginnings of the system in which one goes to hear the singer as much as the music. For quite a time church music developed as polyphony while secular music was developing as melody-and-bass music. Early organ music is therefore contrapuntal which, considering the old term for a fugue (*ricercar*, meaning research), almost means contemplative. This is because of its close association with the church. Pious music for use at home, such as the harmonized metrical psalters of people like Daman, Easte, and Ravenscroft (in the period 1590–1620), exemplified the principle of homophonic counterpoint—the psalm tune (always sung in unison and unaccompanied in church) was supported by four-part counterpoint written largely in first species (note against note) with a bass ingeniously combining significant melody with appropriate emphasis on those degrees of the scale which framed the harmony (the tonic, fifth, and fourth).

It will now be obvious that when melody receives the special attention of listeners, and the supporting bass is regarded simply as part of the background scenery, the relation between rhetoric and reason is in danger of being upset. Two things may happen, and did. One is that a great deal of melody may be supported by an inadequate bass; the other is that the natural growth of music, and therefore of the listener, may be arrested by the use of a bass which is unseasonably primitive. While the primitive is useful for historical study, its use can easily slide over into a deliberate cult of immaturity. At that point the theologian steps in with the comment that the Christian faith is a pilgrimage, not an encampment or a castle.

The typical music of the Restoration period is music of a high sophistication being handled with skill by a series of geniuses. We should say the same of their continental contemporaries, such as Giacomo Carissimi in his cantatas or church operas. It is, we commonly say, *expressive*; we mean rhetorical. There is now a lot of rhetoric to be kept in order. Purcell, Humfrey, Wise, and Jeremiah Clarke could control it. So could Handel, who is the eighteenth century's most puzzling as well as most popular composer. But these composers turned out to be alarmingly imitable. Composers of less intellectual strength could think they were writing the same kind of music when they were doing nothing of the kind. The result in the end was that we called vulgar music, of which the following is a very well loved and very calamitous example:

T. Campbell, c. 1825

And can it be that I___ should___ gain an in - terest___

73

in the___ Sav - vior's blood? Died he for me,___ who caused his pain, for me___ who him___ to death pur - sued? A - maz-ing love, how___ can___ it___ be ____ that thou,___ my God, ____ shouldst die ____ for me? A - maz - ing love: how can it be that thou, my God shouldst___ die for me?

That is a good example of the anthem-hymn form which commended itself to the later English evangelicals. It could never have been written by Handel, but it might not have been written had Handel not lived.

Well loved though it is, it must be criticized for a lack of balance between rhetoric and reason. There are too many notes in the melody for the bass to support. Observe the cadences at the ends of the phrases. Of six cadences, four lead to the tonic in the bass and the other two (though from different directions) lead to the dominant. Observe also that the melody insists on an almost exclusive use of the tonic, dominant, and subdominant chords. Observe, thirdly, the extravagant repetition that the melody requires—two lines of text have to be repeated. Finally, though the melody makes very emphatic use of florid phrases, it is actually made up of very short clauses. Everything there is literate, but it leaves the same impression that a sermon containing much shouting and thumping but little rational discourse leaves. It is oppressive, suffocating of imagination, stultifying of true response, and pretentious. It is, I fear, vulgar. So also is a tune called DIADEM, which is still found in some humnals and comes from the same background.

An alert reader may ask: "Is not the same to be said of another anthem-hymn tune, HELMSLEY ("Lo, he comes with clouds descending")? Nineteenth-century tractarian Anglicans thought it was. They disliked every kind of music in this form for its enthusiastic associations, and *Hymns Ancient and Modern* would not touch it until 1904. But it can be defended on two grounds. The first is that its phrases are longer though its total length, despite melodic flourishes, is more economical, and its effect is enhanced, not diminished, by its use of repetition in the threefold setting of the short line in the verse. This transfers the aesthetic emphasis from the great melodic arch forming its principal phrase to the pathetic repetition of a contrastingly brief rhythm, which is eventually followed by a commanding close:

Second, though it must be admitted that without an adequate bass it is emotionally top-heavy, later composers have provided that bass. (The best contrived bass I take to be that written by Vaughan Williams and included in the *English Hymnal* as Number 7 and in the *Hymnal 1940* as Number 5.) This undoubtedly does for the tune what Bach's basses often did for otherwise intractable primitive chorales, and presents us in the end with the longest hymn tune in existence which contains not a single accidental and yet has not a single engineering flaw. The same arguments would yield the conclusion that of the tunes to "All hail the power of Jesus' name," DIADEM is vulgar and the earlier MILES LANE is as firm as a rock.[1]

[1]Both can be seen in the American *Methodist Hymnal*, 1969 as Numbers 73 and 74 and in the *British Methodist Hymn Book* as Number 91 and Appendix 6.

This line of criticism is partly aesthetic, partly rational. Rhetoric must be controlled if it is not to be oppressive; the vulgar and pretentious is an offence to Christian liberty. Furthermore, a strictly theological argument contends that a craving for uncontrolled rhetoric is a sign of immaturity, and that neither society nor especially the Church should encourage deliberate immaturity. The Gospels leave us in no doubt about our Lord's views on this. If seeking after sensation without responsibility is a sign of immaturity, then what he judged error in Peter's reaction to the transfiguration, and his own reaction to the people who clamored for him to repeat the miracle of the feeding of the five thousand (John 6:22–27) are decisive. So are the demand of the writer to the Hebrews (5:13,14) that his readers be prepared to graduate from milk to solid food and the personal confession of St. Paul in Phil. 3:11–12. The whole matter has been admirably argued by Daniel Jenkins in *Christian Maturity and the Theology of Success*. If the vulgar church music is accused of frustrating growth and encouraging immaturity, it has to face a serious charge indeed. We contend that this is the heart of Christian criticism of church music.

10

Methods of Criticism

A Typical Controversy

At this point I venture on to ground where I tread warily and hope not to offend. I suggest the view, implicit in what I have written so far, that when our preceptors defend the necessity of raising the standard of our church music, they have yet to find a terminology which conforms so clearly with the gospel that it decisively refutes the philistines and the slothful.

Let us examine one or two judgments in the Archbishops' Committee's Report *Music in Church* (1951) and refer to a somewhat truculent criticism of that report made in 1957 by the Bishop of Leicester in diocesan leaflet. The Bishop contended that the values expressed in the Report were those of academic musicians, and as such irrelevant to the needs of parish churches. His protest was written with the gusto that informs the statements of those who would iden-tify themselves with the "plain man." "We find," he wrote at one point, "all the usual stress on the necessity of using music properly constructed from the point of view of composition, and all the silly little points of liturgical purism, such as that there must be no recessional hymn after the blessing, and so on." The Bishop's article contained also a strenuous plea for "popular" music in church.

This, of course, provoked great wrath among the leading musicians of the Church of England. The editor of *English Church Music*, Mr. Leonard Blake, wrote a strong rejoinder in an editorial comment. "To know that there is a God in heaven," he said, "the fountain of all goodness, and not to seek to render to him what is his due is to go the way of eternal damnation. The logical end to the Bishop's argument is to throw up the whole struggle towards better music, decoration, furnishings, or what you will in church, and to let people wallow at whatever levels of taste they were born or have sunk into." On the Bishop's plea for popular music, Mr. Blake wrote, "We would only suggest that when deep religious conviction is truly popular—natural to the folk, if you like—it will find its own music."[1]

The argument was taken up by Dr. Greenhouse Allt, principal of Trinity College of Music, in a lecture to the International Association of Organists at their 1957 conference. "We should tell the Right Reverend the Bishop," said Dr. Allt, "that the cultivated mind of a skilled musician . . . revolts against the use of such a sensuous appeal to replace Church Music, the finest of which is hallowed by tradition, inspired by spiritual experience, and capable of satisfying our deepest spiritual needs when there is an understanding and sympathetic mind ready to receive it. Between the kind of emotion stimulated by the crooner, which the Bishop noted drew the young by the thousand, and the emotion stimulated by Church Music for our religious needs, there is a gulf as wide as that between Lazarus in Abraham's bosom and the souls in torment."[2] Dr. Allt's next paragraph makes it clear that he has been especially stirred to wrath by the sight of Fr. Geoffrey Beaumont's *Folk Mass*.

Let there be no mistake about my opinion. I believe the document that gave occasion for these denunciations is a repulsive piece of ignorant philistinism evincing an attitude of deliberate misunderstanding which is painful in the ill-informed, but catastrophic in the influential. Would that the replies had carried the matter into the Bishop's own ground and been written in theological terms! Responsible and well informed as they are, you can observe that at certain points the replies shy away from the real issue. Mr. Blake said that musicians, if the Bishop were right, might as well throw in the sponge. To this the Bishop would have been entitled to reply, "I *am* right. Do that." When Mr. Blake spoke of the "wallowing" of the ill-informed, the Bishop could have him

[1]Leonard Blake, *English Church Music*, vol. 27, no. 3, pp. 65ff.

[2]Greenhouse Allt, lecture to the International Association of organists, reprinted by M. Hinrichsen, ed., *Organ and Choral Aspects and Prospects* (Hinrichsen, 1958), pp. 49ff.

on the grounds of a lack of pastoral compassion. When he speaks of religious conviction finding its own music, the Bishop could reply, "That is what I observed about the *Billy Graham Song Book.*" The saddest part of Dr. Allt's retort is his appeal that church music is "hallowed by tradition." This is for several reasons very shaky ground on which to stand. If he means that the oldest music is the best, he must mean that we have now lost the art, and the Bishop will get in with a point about Father Beaumont. Possibly he begs a question in referring to the spiritual experience that inspired the best church music. That is a matter of personal biography, and cannot fairly be brought in as evidence. When he speaks of the best music satisfying the spiritual needs of the sympathetic mind, why should not the Bishop and his friends say, "We are not sympathetic minds. We do not accept any of this. Do we then not go to heaven?"

I mention this small controversy largely because it concerned what proved to be a historic musical protest and because it turned on the Archbishops' Committee's Report. It was not in itself of enormous importance, but it did indicate along what lines the musicians defended themselves.

Second, "sensationalism" and "mawkishness" are words of doubtful value. They imply a moralism halfway between permissiveness and theology, a bad stopping place for thinkers and judges. They need some explanatory conjunction with the aesthetic field in which the Report was necessarily written. It should have been possible, says the hostile critic, to find words of clearer meaning which presupposed less sympathy in the reader.

Third, the condemnation of the secular makes us ask at once, "What about the carols?" The precept may be one of decent prudence; it would be an unwise organist who habitually sought the top ten in the charts for the outgoing organ voluntary. But were the churchwardens of Thaxted, England, right in protesting against the display in their parish church of the medieval carol, "Tomorrow shall be my dancing day"? Their argument was that it was a secular poem. Under that head the bishop of the diocese forbade the vicar to display the text, recanting only when the vicar assured him it was a medieval religious song. One tends to wonder whether the bishop knew the difference and, more pertinently, one wonders the same thing about the Archbishops' Committee's Report.

There are, of course, many admirable paragraphs in this document. Dealing with hymn tunes, it says:

> It is because the tunes of songs have the power to conjure an image and an ideal that it is necessary to be sure that the music of hymns does not insinuate a conception of Christ markedly weaker and more limited than the picture of the Incarnate Son of God Revealed in the Bible.[3]

Admirably said! But what images, precisely, are appropriate? The report, when it seeks precision, becomes vaguely levitical:

> The rhythm should have life and movement without levity, and dignity without heaviness. The melody of all the parts, not of the treble only, should be shapely in outline, and neither angular nor dull; in general it should be diatonic, and chromatic intervals should be only sparingly used. The harmony should be for the most part simple, avoiding excessive use of discords which introduce a note of vulgarity or triviality, and which pall with repetition.[4]

In the passage just quoted we have a useful guide for those who want to write new hymn tunes; but it is, as a canon of "Church Music, suitable and unsuitable" (the subhead under which it was written), distressingly imprecise, not to say sentimental. We gather that the Report's authors are quite clear about their own Christian convictions and skillful in diagnosing current diseases (though as later years proved, they were legislating for a remarkably healthy society). But they are not clear about the connection between moral principles and the diagnoses, and so in particular cases they produce judgments which are at best platitudinous and at worst dubious. They commend "dignity without heaviness."

[3]Archbishops' Committee's Report, *Music In Church* (SPCK, 1951), p. 39.
[4]Archbishops' Committee's Report, *Music in Church* (SPCK, 1951) p. 6.

How do you achieve that? How do you make something dignified? They ask for shapely melody in all the parts. Had they asked for good counterpoint we would have known where we were. I feel sure they would have denounced the tenor part in the tune to "Crown him with many crowns". The pleasant tune STOCKTON,[5] which Vaughan Williams harmonized or at least approved, has exactly the same limited compass in its tenor part. They hope things will be neither angular nor dull, so the psalm-tune ST. MARY[6] would probably have to be axed, as would MONTROSE.[7] Chromatic intervals should be sparingly used. That cuts J. S. Bach down to size (unless, perhaps, they meant chromatic intervals in the melody?). As for avoiding discords "which introduce a note of triviality or levity," do they mean that all discords introduce that note or that those which do should be avoided?

If we say the Report, which remains the best of such things available, is defective in being neither theological enough nor musicianly enough, though it is the work of theologians and musicians, the defect is well diagnosed. The following quotation comes from R. E. C. Browne's admirable book *The Ministry of the Word*, in a passage headed "Schizophrenia":

A schizophrenic is not a Jekyll and Hyde personality but a personality so split into isolated fragments that coherent speech and action have died in the death of any single purpose which could be the integrating force of the personality. . . . The term "schizophrenia" will be used here to indicate the condition of a minister of the Word who holds two contradictory sets of doctrines at the same time, one set being unconsciously held and showing itself through the unspoken assumptions which inform parts of his utterances and make for inconsistencies in his pastoral and evangelistic policy. . . .

The "schizophrenic" is the man who tidies up his mind and keeps it tidy; in speech he will tend to be boisterously dogmatic, in the wrong sense of being dogmatic, or he will avoid matters of importance, restricting himself to questions of marginal concern. . . . "Schizophrenia" is avoided by

[5]Number 82 in the *English Hymnal*.
[6]Number 84 in the *English Hymnal*; Number 29 in *Westminster Praise*.
[7]Number 43 in *Westminster*.

forswearing all false simplifications so as to maintain the essential untidiness of mind consequent on the acceptance of Christian doctrine. This essential untidiness is preserved by habitual refusal to come to definite conclusions where there are none, without ever denying the value of either thought so limited or the forms of speech which embody such a doctrinal position.[8]

In that age of pedagogy in church music from 1906–1956 (the terminal dates being the appearance of the *English Hymnal* and the first Beaumont hymn tune), "boisterous dogmatism" was characteristic of the teachers. Nobody who ever knew that doughty fighter for the renaissance of English music, Martin Shaw (1875–1958), could fail to attribute that quality to him—with a strong touch of affection. In his published and spoken views Vaughan Williams, though gentler, had the same quality. Though more solemn in manner, Walford Davies had it too. (I believe this quality is significantly absent from American church musicians of the same period.) It is seen clearly in a pamphlet Martin Shaw wrote at the height of his influence—healthy, muscular, amusing stuff with its heart in the right place.[9] It does, however, contain one intellectually alarming moment when he denounces monotonous melody, overlooking the fact that he himself wrote a tune for "Hark a herald voice is sounding" which begins with seven A's. Boisterous dogmatism is certainly not the mark of a scholar. Although one would hesitate to describe the eminences who contributed to the Report as boisterous, they are often dogmatic, and in consequence often say things of which the opposite is equally true. This is exactly what has bedeviled the whole business of church music criticism during this century.

If there is one point of dogmatism that is especially in danger of damaging the conversation between theologians and musicians today, it is probably the insistence on "nobility" and "dignity" of which the Report's authors are so fond. I believe it is a mistake to regard these as qualities toward which people engaged in Christian worship should *aim*.

[8]R. E. C. Browne, *The Ministry of the Word* (S.C.M. Press, 1954), pp. 42,49.
[9]Martin Shaw, *The Principles of Church Music Composition* (SPCK, 1921)

They are appropriate to a well-ordered coronation service or a bishop's enthronement, when music like Parry's "I was glad" and Richard Dirksen's "Rejoice, ye pure in heart" will be well chosen and will send people away conscious of the dignity of the occasion. However, aiming for dignity will produce empty pomp and those who order such occasions should think not of dignity but of reason. There are other qualities one may rightly hope will be in the minds of people as they leave other kinds of services, such as a weekday evensong in a cathedral, a parish eucharist, or a well-ordered preaching service in a reformed church. Here the effect looked for is contemplativeness, cheerfulness, and integrity. It was too easy in the period 1900–1951 to equate all worship with the most august occasions. The august is, precisely, occasional. Everyday needs are lighter, more down-to-earth.

11

Good and Bad Music

If "down-to-earth" expresses the quality we are seeking in Christian criticism of Christian music, we must at this point return to the New Testament and remind ourselves of the principles we outlined earlier. "Judge not. . . ," says Mt. 7:1; "The spiritual man judges all things but is himself to be judged by no one," says 1 Cor. 2:15. There is no contradiction there. When our Lord, as reported, uses the word "judge," he seems to mean something like "set yourself up as a judge," or perhaps even "speak from a firm assurance of your unanswerable rightness." This kind of behavior, he says, is appropriate to God alone. As St. Matthew compiles his incomparable compendium of dominical moral teaching in Chapters 5–7, this prohibition on judging must be read in the context of a long series of examples which are precise illustrations of how a Christian makes judgments. The ground of these judgments is grace, not law; they are made "in the Kingdom" or, as Paul would say, "in the Lord." Preferring creative love to the mere avoidance of adultery and murder and preferring plain and honest speech to the avoidance of technical perjury is making a judgment, a choice, a distinction. This is a different use of the word judgment from that used in Mt. 7:1, which implies a habit of finding fault with others and asserting one's own superiority. From Paul we gather that a person "in the Lord" will, by virtue of being so, be able to make the right judgments, and that no one can legitimately find fault with him (1 Corinthians 2).

If we set out to make judgments about church music, there are two false trails we may follow. The first, the mere exposure of error, is inadequate. The second, substituting generalized moralism for criticism, is encouraging when positively stated but collapses when one tries to use it for a guide.

It is precisely upon this that the New Testament insists. It is not enough to avoid murder and adultery (though they must be avoided); but neither does our Lord speak of the virtues associated with obedience to God's reign in terms such as "nobility" and "dignity."

Our Lord communicates his teaching by giving pictures of the kind of thing that happens in the Kingdom. These are illustrations of that to which his whole life was dedicated, since he was himself a picture of the Kingdom. On the one hand we have dozens of earthy yet profound parables which describe the ways of God with his people and the perverse ways of the people with God; on the other we have the "signs" in which God's personal presence and spiritual powers disperse devils, heal diseases, and paint a clear picture of what it is like when God's will is his people's delight. The moments are as fleeting as the transfiguration itself, and that is how he designs them to be. They may no more be kept or "frozen" than the manna of the Exodus could be kept overnight. Manna turned to worms if it was kept; the thrill of the moments of illumination would turn sour, humanity being in the condition it is in, if any attempt were made to hold on to it. But the moments are there and illumination is complete while it lasts.

Three things emerge from this which artists have to ponder. First, the communication achieved by any work of art always has a content of transfiguration or thrill; we gasp, sigh, or exclaim, "How beautiful that is!" If that is all we do, the artist's purpose is not necessarily fulfilled; and, conversely, if that is all the artist hopes to get from us, he is not doing his duty as an artist. Just as our Lord firmly resisted people's attempts to offer him empty admiration and usually with a sharp rejoinder tried to deflect their thoughts from him to his Father in heaven (Mark 10:17–18, for example), so it is a meretricious artist whose chief thought is the admiration or reward he or she will receive. Furthermore, just as Jesus would not let people hold onto moments of thrill and transfiguration (Mark 9:5–8, John 6:22–27), so artists who design their work so that thrill or sensation is its chief purpose are defective artists. This is especially obvious in church music, for its purpose is to assist the believer in his journey towards God, not to attach him to the sensations of this world. It is important to notice that this is a general and unalterable aesthetic principle. This is what we meant when we said earlier than an artist has something in mind beyond making a work of art beautiful in the carnal sense. The artist is hoping to contribute to the maturity of whoever reads, hears, or sees his work, to make the beholder more intensely alive. His word shall not return to him void (Isa. 55:11) but shall accomplish that which he purposes, and prosper in the thing to which he sends it.

If this is to be used as a clue to criticism we must take care. It looks as though our criticism would take the form, "This artist's intentions were wrong," or "This is a poor artist." Those are difficult charges to bring, and we should not try to do so unless the evidence from elsewhere is overwhelming. It is possible to say, on the principle that people's natures are known by their fruits, "This is a bad work of art," and so to deduce that on this occasion the artist made a misjudgment. It happens, however, that at certain periods the church was particularly vulnerable to thrill-culture, and from this direction criticism can be brought against many products of evangelical revivals or success phases in the church's history. This was true, for example, in evangelical England in 1800–1850 and the mid-Victorian age in bourgeois protestantism. The overstatement we find in both kinds of music—the verbose anthem-hymn of Methodism and the succulent hymns and anthems of the second-flight Victorian Anglican composers—is an indication of failure on the part of the artist.

A second consequence of our Lord's teaching is that when making a judgment one is not looking for avoidance of error but for creative energy. It is fair to say that we should look for what is best in the best music and celebrate that, rather than spend much time looking for errors in the bad music and warning against that. Error must be identified, but that takes little time and can be disposed of briefly. Distinction must be celebrated, and that is mysterious and unanalyzable.

There have been great periods in church music—in choral music the Tudor polyphonists, the German baroque school, and the English twentieth century; in hymnody the Genevan psalms, the Scottish and English psalms, the baroque chorales, and Vaughan Williams's KING'S WESTON—but how do we make our admiration of these creative? How do we do it with Beethoven, Brahms, or Schubert? We do not say to a student, "Study Beethoven and write like him" or "Study the Genevan psalters and write like that." No, we say, "Study Mozart or Schubert or Berlioz or Stravinsky, or the Scottish Psalter and Crüger and Cyril Taylor and Richard Dirksen, and then write your own music." The proper study of great music will nourish a young artist to *become himself*. Bach admired Pachelbel but did not write Pachelbel. Vaughan Williams studied under Parry, and in 1948 on the centenary of his birth dedicated a motet to his memory. Over it he wrote this inscription: "In the hope that he would have found in this music something characteristic." This is true discipleship. Parry could not have written a note of that motet ("Prayer to the Father of Heaven," one of Vaughan Williams's most profound and mysterious works) but he would have recognized in it something characteristic, not of him, but of his pupil.

Third, perhaps the most obvious point in the recorded teaching of Jesus is that in the Kingdom duty and delight meet. The first Adam destroyed and Christ, the Second Adam, came to restore a condition where what God wills and what delights his creatures is the same. There is no trace in the Gospels of an ethic that equates duty with unpleasantness, or says that righteousness is something from which one wants, or is entitled, to take a holiday. This principle, which always seems in the ordinary fields of moral discourse so remote and ideal, is one artists have always known. If we have overemphasized the point that in important ways artists do not try to make their work beautiful, we can here redress the balance by saying that there is a great deal less temptation for artists to make their work ugly than there is for human beings to make life morally ugly. A composer understands better than most the proposition that duty and delight can be the same thing. Being mortal, the composer is, like everybody else, subject to the law that delight cannot be sought or hoarded. The agonies of creative activity are associated entirely with the artist's consciousness that the kingdom of duty and delight is a real kingdom, but difficult to win. The artist knows it exists; whereas all but a very few people traveling the road of ordinary moral decision believe that what they ought to do is almost certainly what they would rather not do. This is surely a piece of ground upon which theologians and artists can very readily understand one another. It is for this reason that I constantly complain that nobody tells theologians, preachers, or seminarians that they are, by their very nature, artists.

All music stands in and is nourished by a tradition. In church music this point is even more obvious. Church music is doubly under tradition—the tradition of the church and the tradition of music. This means that a word such as "conventional" should be used much more cautiously than it normally is. Conventional usually means "enslaved to tradition" (and of course a Christian must not be content to be enslaved to anything whatever); but what we have lost sight of is the fact that convention also means people meeting each other. In the church people do just that, and the meeting significant for our purpose is the meeting between those who are musical and those who are not. If there is no ground upon which they can agree, church music is useless.

It is important to remember, however, that Christians see their life-style in terms of discipleship. That must mean there are certain freedoms and even spontaneities which they regard as irrelevant to their purpose. Church music will be distorted if its promoters and composers are too preoccupied with humanistic freedom and too insensitive to the demands made by the community. And this community includes not only those visible to us in an identifiable place, but all Christians living now as well as those who have gone before.

It is difficult to find the right word to describe the quality in church music which is conspicuously lacking at present, because all the obvious words have been given a disagreeable tone. Those hostile to the present contention would be happy with "conservative" or "conventional." The best word I can find is "modest." It is clear that the church musician is under limitations which do not beset the secular musician. These limitations need not be disturbing or discouraging. They are the kind of limitations we all experience when in the company of people we do not know very well, which is where the musician often is when writing for the church. In strange company it is necessary to restrain one's natural assertiveness. Between any two or more people there must be a restraining of natural impulses or spontaneity, for once these restraints are withdrawn civilized life cannot continue. Assertiveness talks; modesty listens. The best church musicians have always been the best listeners. When the precentor of Coventry Cathedral writes so memorably in his booklet *Evensong in Coventry Cathedral* that the church's worship is "a conversation which began long before you were born and will continue long after you are dead," he is saying exactly what we need at this moment. The great church musician listens to the conversation already going on before joining in it.

There is a tendency at present, which has been with us more than twenty years, for church music to break in on the conversation and make gestures comparable to a person bursting into a room and stopping everyone present that he may assert himself. All music which self-consciously adopts a style is like a person who puts on airs. It is affected and overbearing. I am afraid that in the experience of most of us this affectation is called "popular." That has come to mean the productions of the Light Music School in England and of many groups in America associated with the young, from whom the American Catholics have suffered more than most. Not infrequently they are put up to it by trendy clergy, but the fact is that the movements are often associated with youth.

We should, of course, equally criticize the behavior of the old who callously interrupt the not-to-be interrupted or contradicted young, but in the history of church music this does not happen often. Because of the shape of history it is the new which bursts in on the old. But the same principle holds either way: the Church is conducting a conversation to which it is wise to listen before one contributes. If one does not, the effect is one of boorish interruption.

But note, before we proceed, that one does not adversely criticize music in a jazz idiom, or a light idiom, or any of the popular idioms, because it is jazz, light, popular, youthful, or modern. One criticizes it only to the extent that it is immodest, discourteous, uncivilized, or ill-made. In every category of modern popular church music I find exceptions which absolutely forbid moralistic generalizations about it. We criticize affected and assertive music; in this category I would put Malcolm Williamson's setting of "Jesu, lover of my soul." On the other hand, I would put his setting of Psalm 121 in the category of modest, unaffected music which we can always use.

A composer who is a good listener in the sense we are assuming will compose church music which, if it is choral, will mean something to the unmusical while commanding the respect of the musical. It will fittingly take its place in an activity whose chief object is not musical. That is where the Tudor choral composers and the baroque composers so often score over the Victorians. There was always a danger of a certain operatic quality taking over the texture of Victorian choral music. The operatic is not in itself inappropriate to the Christian religion; Verdi's *Requiem* surely proves that. But a certain quasi operatic plushness about the typical anthem, popular in the early 1900's in England and America, repels a sensitive critic because it *interrupts* and distracts from the church's true conversation. Later composers in both countries recovered from this malady with surprising success.

Writing music for unmusical people to sing actually amounts to composing folk songs; and it is not surprising to discover how many successful hymn tunes have been composed by ministers of religion. They knew what it was like to stand in a pew and sing. Organists have done it admirably when they too had this remembrance. The person who cannot compose what ordinary people can sing is the musician who, while excellent in any other musical respect, has forgotten or never knew what hymn singing is like for the singer. It is no accident that except for the magnificent KING'S WESTON, Vaughan Williams's hymn tunes written after 1906 neither gained nor deserved the popularity of the four he wrote for the *English Hymnal* (the tunes to "For all the saints," "Come down, O love divine," "God be with you," and "Hail thee, festival day"). He drifted away from the worship of the congregation fairly soon after 1906. It is no accident that J. B. Dykes, a parish parson, wrote the large number of acceptable tunes for which he is still well known. It is no accident that of John Stainer's compositions, his best music is found in one Anglican chant (E minor) and two or three hymn tunes; for Stainer, as all those who revere his memory insist, was at his best when he was encouraging music out of others. It is not only a question of writing less music than one would otherwise write, nor is it a matter of rebelliously accepting the limitations of the unmusical community. It is a matter of liking the people who are going to sing the hymns, and that means "welcoming the duty" in a truly Gospel sense. Some people who write successful hymn tunes write nothing else, or nothing else that endures. Hymn-tune writers are essentially strolling players who interpret with affection the mood of ordinary people, and when they do it well they enlarge those people.

It could be argued that musicians who are at any point self-conscious, or even censorious in their relation to congregations, do this less happily. It is most interesting to note after the lapse of years that only two or three tunes by Martin Shaw, that great crusader for the revival of English music, have achieved greatness and popularity (MARCHING, PURPOSE, and LITTLE CORNARD). Stanford, a great teacher and a dedicated churchgoer, rarely succeeded in writing folk music; even his most singable tunes are musicians' music to some extent. One respectfully doubts whether any of Herbert Howells's hymns will achieve rugged popularity except the relatively early MICHAEL ("All my hope on God is founded"), which became popular more than thirty years after it first appeared. By contrast, the tune ABBOT'S LEIGH ("Glorious things of thee are spoken"), popular in Britain within ten years of its composition in 1937 and beginning to make its way in America, proclaims its composer a hymn-tune writer worthy to stand among the greatest.

Hymns are derived from the community to a very large extent and in the end cannot be composed by people who do not positively like the people who sing them. A good hymn tune is about 10 per cent original and 90 per cent traditional. It cannot succeed if it says nothing new, or if what it says is said unintelligibly, frowningly, or pompously.

There is, however, a most important corollary of the truth

that the community produces the music, hymns or choral. If a good musician must listen to the church's conversation before writing a contribution to it, what is he or she going to hear? Take the example of Arthur Sullivan (1841-1900), who is the most extraordinary phenomenon in English church music.

Sullivan is considered to have been the finest musical craftsman alive in Britain in his age. By an incalculable margin, more of his music is played and enjoyed a hundred years after its composition than of any other nineteenth-century English composer. For proportion, harmony, and good taste, there is nothing in the period to touch Sullivan's operas. But when one turns to his church music, one finds a failure of taste as consistent as his judgment in secular works was faultless. The *Festival Te Deum* is good for nothing but a hearty laugh, oscillating as it does between material that would have gone happily on to the Savoy stage ("We therefore pray thee, help thy servants") and material that for sheer flatulent pretentiousness is even in that age hard to beat. (When this great composer wrote bad music, he wrote it to professional standards.) *The Golden Legend*, with the once celebrated chorus "O gladsome Light," containing a coda that is hardly an advance on that celebrated religious piece of his, *The Lost Chord*, is another beautiful example. So was the well-known anthem "I will mention the lovingkindness of the Lord." It needs no argument; it is one long butter-slide. But why? Can we come to any other conclusion than that the conversation Sullivan overheard in the church was precisely of this standard? The values he picked up from whatever church he knew must have been the values of the most inane of bourgeois drawing rooms.

I think the same kind of case could be made for Michael Haydn and for Felix Mendelssohn. At the risk of offending his many admirers, I cannot refrain from the judgment that there is more authentic music in one measure of the *Serious Variations* or the *Midsummer Night's Dream* than in twenty pages of the *Hymn of Praise*.

A church produces the music it wants and deserves. You can tell much about the ethos of a church—again I mean not its leaders but the people who hear and join in church music—from the quality of music it most freely accepts and approves. Sir Thomas Beecham, a master of perverse epigram, went on record as saying that all composers do their worst work for the church. That as a generalization is preposterous—Bach, Handel, Beethoven, and Vaughan Williams being exceptions that demolish it. But insofar as the statement is true, it is simply not the composers' fault. When they took the trouble to ask the question, the church provided a miserable answer. When they wrote without asking the question, they made a virtue out of what should never have been a necessity and produced masterpieces which the ordinary churchgoer knew nothing about.

The composer, then, who listens well to good conversation will be inspired to produce his or her best for the church. If the church seems to be demanding pretentious or "thrill" music, the composer will either go and write for somebody else, or will succumb to the temptation to write what any composer can write easily enough. If the royalties offered for these low-grade productions are high enough, the musician is understandably under great pressure. One thing we are entitled to conclude: despite the attacks made on the twentieth-century church in our time, mostly by people whom that church has supported, encouraged, and made articulate, the evidence of twentieth-century church music suggests that at an important level the church is a great deal healthier than it was in many parts of the world a hundred years ago. Let the theologians make what they can of *that*.

12

Good and Bad Music Making

There is a scene in the Gospels in which the disciples
failed to cure an epileptic boy, and our Lord diagnosed their
failure as overlooking the fact that this kind of thing is done
only by prayer (Mark 9:29; some authorities say "by prayer
and fasting"). Prayer, with or without fasting, sounds a shade
forbidding; but it is what we have been dealing with when we
mentioned the artist's duty and delight with respect to the
ongoing conversation of the Church. Prayer, it is generally
held, is lateral as well as vertical communication, as supernatural in the one dimension as in the other. The tiny
miracle of healing people through church music needs
exactly this preparation.

Sentimentality

Before going on to more practical matters, we must say
something about sentimentality, that vice with which disre-
putable church music is often charged. Sentimentality can
be described as taking a short-cut to sensation that bypasses
responsibility. One of its most common forms is imitation.
There is another symbolic story in the Gospels in which
Peter, seeing his Master walking on the water, immediately
plunged in and sank. Disregarding what my American
friends would amiably call the logistics of this affair, the
teaching it imparts is quite clear. It is not enough for Peter to
go through the external motions he sees his Master making,
any more than reciting the words they had heard the Master
use enabled the other disciples to heal the epileptic. Something further is required. Jesus made it as clear as he could
that this, on certain conditions, would be available to those
who believed in him, but that during his own lifetime they

94

did not have it. The coming of the Holy Spirit (foretold in detailed terms in St. John 14–16) was in fact the announcement that they had begun the process of achieving it. The "it" we speak of is indescribable—we really know only the difference between its presence and its absence by comparing the behavior of the Twelve before Pentecost with the behavior of eleven of them after it. The nearest we can get (without traveling on a long theological journey) is to call it a kind of communication between people and God and, in consequence, between people and each other. There is all the difference in the world between this and mere imitation. Imitation is superstitious and in the worst sense magical. It is the pattern of behavior by which a woman thinks that if she imitates a film star's hair style she will acquire her sex appeal, or a man thinks that the purchase of a new car will gain him the esteem and respect of his neighbors. That is a form of sentimentality.

Pretentiousness, often nauseating, is a form of sentimentality generated through imitation. And as we noted earlier, there is a fine line between pretentiousness and legitimate rhetoric. But at the other end nothing could be plainer. The great fault of insecure musicians is striving after effect, imitating an effect somebody else achieved, without the needful "prayer and fasting," which can mean simply that the musician isn't technically up to what he has attempted. A choir may perform music casually that ought to be performed with precision; an organist may be too spiritually minded to play the right notes; and a composer may strive after effect without taking note of the musical hazards he or she may encounter. For example, the chromaticism which frightened the authors of the Archbishops' Committee's Report is to be interpreted as the work of a composer who thinks that by using the chords Beethoven used he can write like Beethoven. The sentimental quality in a hymn tune is the casual use of expressive effects which in the hands of masters like Schubert and Brahms can be immensely moving by people who overlook the exquisite sense of proportion and the ruthless contrapuntal integrity that Schubert and Brahms always show.

It might be argued that none of this does much harm; that

95

if people want to go on singing F. C. Maker's tune to "Dear Lord and Father of mankind," still universally popular in America though it is English, they should be allowed to do so. I cannot agree. When Vaughan Williams wrote that good taste is a moral concern (in the preface to the *English Hymnal*, 1906), I am with him and I think the church should be. Failures of taste are ultimately failures of nerve; bad taste argues insecurity, competitiveness, and a lust for quick results. Walk on the water in that spirit and you'll sink.

But bad taste can also be failure of reason. It is within most readers' knowledge that local churches of all denominations in both our countries are much given nowadays to customs which have precious little authority or precedent and about which questions are never asked. The same people will know that if a question is asked, research is pursued, and the conclusion is reached that the custom ought to be altered, a local church authority may nonetheless, in defiance of reason and evidence, insist in keeping it. As I turn aside to give one clear example of this, I ask the reader to remember that I am using it as an illustration of the fundamental fear of reason, fear indeed of inconvenient truth, which is another facet of sentimentality.

Amen

I refer therefore to the custom of singing "Amen" at the end of all hymns. The story is this.

There are two authentic uses of amen—the asserverative and the responsive. The first is as it appears in solemn sayings of our Lord as recorded in the Gospels, beginning in English, "Verily, verily. . . ," which is in Greek "Amen, amen." It is used to introduce, not conclude, a statement of special importance. The other use is as a response by people in whose name or to whom something has been said. This is the only liturgical use of the word, and it is of the greatest importance. It is here part of a conversation (as in 2 Cor. 1:18–22). In ancient times it was used this way in worship, where people responded to prayers, and especially to the great prayer at the eucharist, with a solemn and loud

"Amen," meaning "We are associated with that." It is heard sometimes less formally but even more intensely where people in some congregations interject "amen" when the preacher's words echo their own convictions. At any time when one voice says a prayer and all voices respond, the simplest and most ancient response is "amen."

The use of this word at the end of a hymn which everybody has sung has therefore, at first sight, no justification whatever. But the custom has an origin which has deceived many people into considering it a modern necessity. The fact is that all the ancient Ambrosian hymns end with a trinitarian doxology followed by "Amen." It is believed that Ambrose himself composed songs for orthodox Christians to sing in reply to certain songs invented and sung in a belligerent spirit by the unorthodox Arians, who at this time (the later fourth century) were in open conflict with the orthodox. It may therefore have been the custom for some to sing the hymn, and all within earshot to sing a responsive "Amen"— "That's what we all believe about the Trinity" (the point largely in dispute).

Ambrosian hymnody, however, very soon developed in monastic settings rather than controversial ones, and here we are on firm ground—their plainsong tunes always included an amen after the doxology, which still always stood at the end. It is reasonably certain that liturgically these office hymns (as they came to be called—hymns of the "office" or routine daily worship) were sung antiphonally. We should not by any means assume that the doxology was sung by all present, but we can more safely assume that the amen was.

However, the whole nature of hymnody changed at the Reformation. There was no question of singing amen at the end of hymns in Luther's time (nor has there ever been such a tradition in the German-speaking churches). The *Gloria* did not appear in the Genevan Psalter, though it was included in the English and Scottish psalters presumably for optional use; but no amen is appended to that in the early editions.

In fact, in the English and early American system of hymnody, amen is never sung after hymns until the mid-nineteenth century. Isaac Watts and Charles and John Wesley knew nothing of it. What brought it back was the revived interest in medieval hymnody aroused in England by the Oxford Movement from 1833 onward, generating a wave of translation from the Latin which eventually made the whole Sarum system of Latin hymnody available in English. The doxologies, with their amens, were included in the translations.

So eager were the Tractarians to make it clear that the medieval culture alone was the pure religious culture, and medieval hymnody the proper norm for all other hymnody, that at a number of points in their hymnals they appended doxologies with amens to existing hymns. The most notorious instance was the adding of a spurious doxology to "When I survey the wondrous cross," but there were many others. Doxology or no, amen was added to every hymn, and since virtually every non-plainsong tune in that book ended with a perfect cadence the amens were set uniformly to a plagal cadence. This hymnal was the most famous of all humnals, the 1861 edition of *Hymns Ancient and Modern*.

The custom spread through Anglican hymnals and was imitated by the Congregationalists and Presbyterians, and to a limited extent by the Methodists and Baptists, for no reason but the obscure and irrational notion that the Church of England knew its work in matters of liturgy. Around 1920 the Anglicans recognized that adding amens had been an anarchronism and an error, and began to abandon them. Obediently the nonconformists followed them at about a twenty-year interval, and by about 1950 the amen on hymns had virtually disappeared in England, although it was retained for some time in Scotland.

Now consider what a patchwork of misunderstanding and anachronism all this is. Singing amen after post-Reformation hymns was unknown before about 1850. There is no older precedent for it, it was in any case an error, and those who initiated it have long repented of it. It is an excellent example of a custom which people still jealously guard in America, any criticism of which arouses great indignation, and any argument against which is disregarded. When by a series of accidents the minister and organist of one Presbyterian Church heard the arguments against it and expressed themselves in favor of acting on them, the church solemnly decreed by congregational meeting, in the year 1976, that it must be retained.

This malignant irrationality is, of course, the chief enemy of all who seek to make judgments on rational grounds. It precludes any possibility of making judgments on any higher ground such as we are here suggesting. We can return now to our main argument, which we left at the point where we identified a relationship between sentimentality and the deliberate disregard of inconvenient truth.

The Organist and the Organ

A 1922 report of the Archbishops' Committee on Church Music wisely warned that the organist has at his command an instrument "of greater depth, power, range, and variety of tone than any other." Even a small organ is an instrument of considerable power in relation to the building in which it stands unless it is deliberately voiced very quietly. No musician is from the beginning placed in a position of so much potential power over others as is the organist. A virtuoso pianist is restrained by the ascetic discipline required to attain a concert standard. The most eminent of conductors is restrained by the need to establish an intimate and vital relation with the orchestra members. But the organist, without making any effort at all, without any practice, without the possibility of being restrained by anything but an explosive upsurge of public opinion, can make more physical noise and exercise more affective power over other people than anybody.

Therefore the musician who would handle the organ is especially obliged to see the discipline along strictly ascetic lines. The very nature of the instrument is against his producing a musically good and religiously edifying performance on it. The organist must restrain all those impulses to exercise irresponsible power which the instrument itself and its position over against the congregation arouse.

In 1951 the Reverend Romilly Micklem, a distinguished preacher, told a congregation of organists that nothing so completely "gives you away" as the way in which a musician plays the organ. To hear a series of organists accompany a service, aside from the acknowledged virtuosi (so many of whom reside in America), is to look at a case history of psychological maladjustments. It is in service playing, especially hymn playing, that this appears because it is there that the player has to make so many decisions which have nothing to do with the actual playing of the notes. Let none disparage the amateur organist who, except in America, is so essential to the continuance of church music; we say only that a professional has usually learned to dissemble what the amateur has had no opportunity of even knowing about. Nor are professionals immune from the generalization, for their service playing can, in contrast to that of the benevolent British amateur's tendency to overstatement, be so "buttoned up" that it suggests a person who dare not open his mouth in public for fear of giving away some guilty secret.

One may suspect that psychiatrists take too little advantage of the possibilities of organ playing for revealing psychological conditions. Very broadly, evidences of maladjustment to which I have become accustomed are (I here speak of Britain; America will not be ignored) overemphasis on 16-foot pedal tone and 8-foot reed tone. The reasons are not at all recondite. Loud reed tone is the most dramatic of the tone colors that an organ produces—it suggests trumpets, which have always been the most evocative of all instruments. Deep pedal tone has a double purpose: it imparts a sense of security and discreetly covers up the vagaries of the left hand. Therefore every good organ teacher tells his or her pupils to be sparing of splashy reed effects and trains pupils on Bach trios with an uncompromising 8-foot pedal.

Perhaps the age of malignant amateurism is beginning to pass away, but one may still hear in some places an organist who seeks grand effects at cut rate who plays the D Minor Toccata without its Fugue, who covers up deficiencies of articulation by using a subfoundational manual stop, who plays impressive-sounding pieces without really playing a single measure correctly. It is not altogether to this organist's misfortune that many church organs built fifty or more years ago were designed to minister to these temptations; they were usually designed to specifications provided by people like him.

Therefore what is called the baroque movement in organ-craft has rendered a signal service in uncovering a whole series of psychological conditions in organists, especially in Britain. The interested reader should look up the correspondence in the musical press of 1951 concerning the organ then newly installed in London's Festival Hall, and notice the passionate denunciations and frantic—certainly irrational—tirades which lovers of the old "romantic" organ were moved to write about it. The old-fashioned roll and thunder had given place to a ruthless clarity which enabled the listener to hear and obliged the player to play precisely what was written. From a country in which any recital in the 1930s might well contain an organ transcription of an orchestral movement all these majestic sounds were to be swept away; the King of Instruments was dethroned.

Nobody can be seriously out of sympathy with what these English innovators attempted and what they can now be seen to have achieved. Least of all will American organists be out of sympathy, for in this country the so-called baroque revival has had a far more generous exposure. Certain parts of the United States have, of course, greater affinities with the European countries from which classic organs came than with Britain itself, and the presuppositions of the classical style are more or less taken for granted by builders, teachers, and players alike.

But a strange thing has accompanied this new attitude in organ building. There is a widened cleavage between the two aspects of organ playing which is obscured by the foregoing categorization of organists as amateurs or professionals. It is near the truth to say that the baroque revival of organ building is a primarily professional ethic. It is quite certainly a recital ethic. The primary virtue of an organ built in the classical style is always advertised by its exponents as contrapuntal clarity, and quite rightly so. This is a quality appreciated by a listener to organ music, which is church music only accidentally because one must normally go inside a church to hear it. Organ solo music is, with the solitary exception of the organ mass of the baroque period, right on the periphery of liturgical music.

The difference between solo recital playing and service playing is now very considerable, much wider than it used to be. Service playing demands a great deal of imagination on the player's part, and has very little to do with the fundamentalist obedience to a score that recital playing of the modern kind requires. An organist must constantly edit a score; very few anthem scores are scored for organ on three staves, and of course no hymn tunes are so scored. When accompanying anthems and service settings the organist gets no instructions about registration, and sometimes indeed has to play from a piano reduction of what was originally an orchestral score (as, for example, in any Handel or Restoration anthem or a festive piece like Parry's "I was glad"). The decisions are different from and more subtle than those demanded for a performance of the work of Bach, where the instructions are conventional rather than explicit, or works of the French composers, who usually provide instructions very carefully.

Hymns are another matter, for here the organist usually has a four-part vocal score to accompany, or if not that, a two-stave song setting, and the player must play the same score from three to seven times. Moreover, the singing body the player is accompanying is an untutored and unrehearsed body which, in many cases, knows the tune by heart but needs to be encouraged to sing.

The musical ethos of many choral pieces and hymns requires a different approach from that demanded by baroque composers, much of whose work is scored properly for organ continuo and other instruments. There is no such thing, in musical terms, as a baroque hymn tune. Chorales composed during the baroque period are treated in all hymnals like any other hymn tunes.

None of this is greatly advantaged by an organ tone specially devised for the communication of counterpoint to a listener. It is greatly impeded by a certain kind of classical organ—the repressive kind designed so as to make the performance of anything but baroque or modern French music impossible. The most obvious repressive measure is the omission of swell boxes, so that no part of the organ is "under expression." It is impossible on such a machine to have infinite gradations of unchanging tone. All gradations are achieved in what is known nowadays as terraced dynamics. For the accompaniment of any church music not founded in a baroque musical ethos such an instrument is useless; and these instruments' existence implies a judgment that such music simply ought not to be performed at all. I contend that this is an unjustifiable prohibition even from the recitalist's point of view; but for purposes such as accompanying many respectable anthems, or psalms sung to Anglican chant at evensong, it is totally out of place.

For accompanying hymns the difficulties are different. Terraced dynamics are by no means out of place here; crescendos and diminuendos of the subtle romantic kind are out of place. But the difficulty with some such organs, especially when they are small, is that it is less easy than it used to be to devise different forms of *forte* or *mezzo-forte*, not much different in volume but different in tonal texture. Since a classical instrument relies heavily on "upperwork" for its clarity, and in producing any considerable volume of tone is almost impotent without its mutations and mixtures, it follows that during a hymn this kind of sound is being made all the time. It is not very widely recognized by professionals how tiring to the ear and discouraging to the singers a persistent use of very high registers can be. We have to add to this another habit which has probably been inculcated by the professional ethic of limiting registration changes in classical organ music to the fewest possible (partly because on very old organs there was not much chance of changing stops without great effort or even without leaving the bench). This leads to the remarkable phenomenon of organists playing a whole hymn on an unvarying registration, with not the least attention to its words or to the elemental surge of sound that a congregation naturally produces as it "warms up."

It is not pleasant to have to say it, but observation has persuaded me that the better the technical equipment organists have, the less likely they are to play hymns in a manner that encourages congregations to sing. And this, if it is true, is probably because organists nowadays, and perhaps especially in America where playing standards are so enviably high, simply regard the organ as an instrument for doing things quite different from those for which we used to think it was made. The organ is becoming less and less an instrument for the reassurance and edification of worshiping congregations and more and more an instrument for the performance of recitals.

These are only tendencies, and while questions ought to be asked about them at the highest professional level, I do not contend that they ought to be totally reversed or that the classical organ design is impossible to integrate with sensitive and edifying service playing. Organs need not be aggressively voiced in dead buildings; organists need not be so contemptuous of the church's popular music; hymnals need not be so printed that stanza shapes and thought shapes in hymn texts are totally obscured (though it will take a major revolution to do anything about that in America now). What I here gently warn against is the real danger that professionals will fail altogether to "listen to the conversation." There are many church musicians who are musicians operating by accident in church; this is the occupational hazard of a musical milieu so culturally opulent as that of the United States. Just as there is always a danger that composers will stop listening, or be tempted to write before they listen, and thus fail to write edifying church music, so the same may happen to organists and, *mutatis mutandis*, to choir directors. It is a very curious thing, providing an odd kink in our argument, that we may be asking here for a modesty that will strike some professionals as being exactly the opposite. For dull, uninspired, and insensitive playing in services is not modesty, even though it may be the product of a scholarly devotion to the text of recital music. It is not modesty but a surly taciturnity, and that is not what we are after.

The classical organ achieves its clarity by carefully blending tones at different pitches to produce a single audible tone; the mutations and mixtures, when properly voiced, do not confuse the contrapuntal lines, but clarify them. That is the whole principle. A pure tone is the most confusing sort of tone; a complex tone is crystal clear—you get clear counterpoint when in physical fact pipes of six or seven different pitches, including fifths and octaves, are sounding. This paradox is familiar to all modern recitalists. By the same token, one may well achieve a clearer, more rhythmical, and more encouraging accompaniment of a simple hymn tune by radical modification of the written score than by fundamentalist obedience to it. Here I do not mean altering the bass and varying the harmonies (a quite different subject upon which I shall touch in a moment); I mean redistributing the notes, giving important attention to phrasing, and occasionally—very important—introducing momentary silences. Here are several fragments which show what an organist who knows how to make people sing can get away with once a congregation has warmed up through singing a couple of stanzas. In each case the use of the rests can be the best encouragement of all.[1]

Sicilian Mariners

Lancashire

The point here is that the organist must translate the hymn score into organ language as he or she plays. This will be not a distraction but a reassurance for the congregation,

[1]The harmonies presupposed in both cases are those in the Presbyterian Hymnbook, 1955.

especially if the organist's chief attention is to rhythm and touch, to the use of detached pedal here and there, to detached melody, or detached inner parts with legato melody, and all other refinements he or she has mastered in playing organ music. It is quite possible to abandon the notion that *fortissimo* throughout is the only way to keep a congregation together. This unfortunate habit of playing very loudly all the time probably comes in America from the need in the past to support very large congregations in very dead churches.

Alternatives to the Organ

A word may be expected here on the vexatious question of whether the electronic organ is an adequate substitute for a pipe organ in places where financial resources are insufficient to make a pipe organ possible. It would be better to enclose our thoughts on this in a general discussion of whether there is any alternative nowadays to a pipe organ for congregational accompaniment.

The conceivable alternatives are, one supposes, a piano, guitars, or an orchestra. A judgment made by Pope Pius X in 1903 on the piano was as downright as it was surprising:

> The employment of the piano is forbidden in church, as is also that of noisy or frivolous instruments.such as drums, bells, cymbals, and the like.[2]

The piano is, surely, a better instrument for accompanying a reasonably small group than that terrible invention which English people so insultingly call the American organ (in the United States it is known as a pump organ, and its invention and existence are decisive evidence of the inherent sinfulness of human nature). The piano is rhythmical, sensitive, and flexible. But two things are against it. One is that its inability to sustain tone without the use of the sustaining pedal causes it to become ineffective in a building, or in support of a congregation, of any considerable size, and

[2]*Catholic Church Music* (1933), p. 10, par. 19.

the other is that the need to re-edit the vocal score of a hymn is much more urgent than it is in the case of the organ, partly to keep the rhythm going through long sustained melody notes (as for example in "Holy, holy, holy"). This demands considerable skill in the performer and leaves room, if the skill is less than the zeal, for a good deal of vulgarity.

The guitar, so popular nowadays as an alternative, is a lamentable substitute for several reasons. In the first place the guitar is by nature a gentle instrument, and the need to amplify it (or a group of guitars) to make it adequate as support for a congregation seriously distorts its nature. Another difficulty is that variety of tone is simply not available. Third, there is always a tendency for arrangers to produce exceedingly ugly harmonic progressions, such as are sometimes provided in modern hymnals, which damage the apprehensions of listeners. This is probably due to the fact that the guitar, like the organ in England, is an instrument which it is legitimate to play very badly in public. The provision of any kind of decent contrapuntal bass, such as is written in any decent hymn tune, takes the music beyond the capacities of players who are accustomed to the quite different harmonic conventions of secular pop music. A fourth reason is the inevitable danger that guitarists will contemptuously dismiss the need to learn a proper accompaniment style in the manner we have just demanded from well-trained church organists. In many ways the associations of this instrument are all wrong. Its sound tends to bring into church the atmosphere of callous slovenliness and emotional brainwashing which in secular life it has made so much its own. Here I think Pope Pius X was right, though his latter-day children apparently believe otherwise.

The orchestra is a different problem. Naturally we do not often hear it, although at the time of writing a certain famous (and immense) congregation in Dallas, Texas, provides a full orchestra for its service every Sunday. While the instrument that can play Brahms's Fourth Symphony is obviously not to be dismissed as improper in itself, two things are against its use for public worship. Whether the band is small or large, we are going to get the same invariability of sound—which in playing successive stanzas of a hymn we insist is depressing—that we get from guitars or the pump organ, unless somebody does a great deal of arranging. Hymns are simply not orchestral music by nature. The other more important objection is that a large orchestra suggests a triumphalism which we cannot but think inappropriate. Public worship is not in *that* sense a grand occasion, and the sense in which it is a grand occasion may easily be obscured by the presence of a playing body which one normally associates with the highest of "high culture." What the guitar brings into church in the way of inappropriate associations from one direction, the large orchestra brings from another. If the occasion is very grand and festive and unusual, like a coronation or a special festival of church music, the orchestra is less inappropriate, though its contribution to the grandeur, its diminishing of the penitence that must always precede true wonder and delight, remains even there a questionable advantage. These grand religious occasions are spiritually indigestible and should be for that reason very infrequent.

The use of occasional orchestral instruments or of small reinforcing groups (Brass groups alone are practicable) brings the thing down to manageable size, and provided this is still kept for an occasion of special festivity it is not objectionable but edifying, because the proportion of the occasion is not too much distorted.

This brief discussion may serve to rehabilitate the slightly damaged reputation of the organ itself. The truth is that all substitutes for the organ in the accompanying and decorating of public worship are more restricted in their usefulness. A well-built organ, large or small, provides resources which all the others miss. But this means that much more depends on the player's decision; therefore the organ is more easily abused than any of the alternatives. This is a position with which Christians should be content. *Corruptio optimi pessimum*—the Christian life-style is the most dangerous of all, since it is always possible for the Christian to misuse resources whose range is incomparably greater than those of any other faith. We therefore express discontent when we encounter in organists either vulgar exhibitionism or sullen detachment.

This brings us to the electronic instrument, which can be regarded as an alternative to the organ. There are some who wish that electronic keyboard instruments were given a name other than "organ" so that comparisons between these and pipe organs could be more objective. To call them organs suggests that they are usurpers.

The basic proposition must be this: there is no inherent inferiority in the electronic principle of sound production. This is normally overlooked by the defenders of the pipe organ. It is no legitimate accusation to say that the electronic organ produces sound by technological means. So does the pipe organ. So, you must admit, does the violin. All humanly made instruments harness physical principles to specific human uses, and that is technology. The question does not turn on the inalienable property of the pipe organ to be better than the electronic instrument. The question is whether *this* electronic instrument serves the purpose better than *this* pipe organ. Inductive generalizations with moral overtones are invariably pernicious. In order to say "All electronic organs are bad organs" you must prove that there is something inseparable from the nature of electronic sound production which precludes such an instrument from giving an agreeable sound, or as good a sound as a pipe organ. Otherwise there is no difference between the attitude of mind that produces the proposition "All electronic organs are unsatisfactory"—meaning, "I am certain beyond correction that the next one I meet will be unsatisfactory"—and the mind which says "All football players are dumb" or "All publishers are unreliable," which similarly means that this is what you determine to predicate of the next football player or publisher you meet.

That said, I now admit that of almost every electronic organ I have encountered I have said, "*This* one is unsatisfactory." But I have a suspicion that the electronic production of tone is just like all the inventions of the twentieth century (in contrast with inventions of the nineteenth) in that because of the oddly demonic character of our age they have gone wrong and rendered as much disservice as benefit. Some historian will explain this, no doubt. The electronic instrument suffers not only from the inherent difficulty (I refuse yet to say "impossibility") of producing good tone, but also from the environment into which it was born—the pop culture, the greedy society, and cut-rate ethic. Electronic organs can be remarkably cheap, and can feed the lust for pretentiousness which disfigures so much of modern bourgeois society. People give rudimentary instruments of this kind to their children for Christmas. This must be recognized and then dismissed from our consideration, because it is an accident, not a property of this kind of instrument.

There is, of course, no disputing the repulsiveness of the glutinous sounds produced by mass-produced electronic instruments for popular entertainment. The worst excesses of the organs of fifty years ago, against which musicians used to protest with horror, are Schantz and Harrison compared with the deliberately distorted noises we get from behind the bar or within the pop band or, we must add, from the public address systems of famous evangelical crusade meetings. The merest suspicion of this is enough to induce in church people an uneasy feeling that the worst of the secular world is creeping in on them. We add to that the too-easy availability of instruments without full pedalboards, or with an octave of toe-bars, compensated with devices like chimes and vibrators and echo-gadgets, and we certainly have an instrument appropriate to the support of whatever hymns they sing in hell.

But that aside, what are the objective advantages and disadvantages of the electronic organ? Cheapness is normally the most important, actually the most delusive. Churches sometimes install these instruments for the wholly spurious reason that the less money is spent on music the better the church will be. The answer to that nonsense, especially when it is piously claimed that the church gives to missions what it withholds from music, is that music is part of the church's mission. And it is actually true that an electronic instrument designed with the needful care and skill can be quite expensive. Still, there is not much that is healthy in the argument that this way you can get a good deal more for a lot less expense.

Adaptability is a more solid advantage. Churches are

often still designed so that there is nowhere to put the organ without either stifling its sound or drowning out the congregation. The allocation of space for ranks of pipes is a greater problem than the setting of speakers.

By far the most solid advantage of the electronic organ is relative portability. This affects the British more than Americans. Far more British congregations than American feel that the days of their present physical sanctuary (which may be old, expensive to maintain, unadaptable to modern worship, and geographically ill-sited) are numbered. There is a *prima facie* case, in such circumstances, when an old pipe organ has become unplayable, for installing an electronic instrument. The presence of a new and excellent pipe organ might present a weighty argument in favor of retaining the old premises, whereas the electronic can be moved with little more difficulty than a piano plus a hi-fi system.

It is therefore in unstable or pioneer situations that electronic instruments have their most legitimate market. This prompts an uneasy feeling that the installation of magnificent new pipe organs argues an absence of that pilgrim or pioneer mentality which should actually never be totally forgotten by settled Christian congregations. But the question then is whether in one's zeal for pilgrimage one must sacrifice musical taste.

To be fair, I ask those who dismiss the musical possibilities of electronics to hear either the continuo organs (used by several leading British musical groups) or the four-manual church organ at St. James's Church, Newcastle upon Tyne, before making up their minds. These emerge from a tiny factory in North London where the firm of Copeman Hart, Ltd., gets as near as possible to designing these instruments with the loving care and musical sensitivity with which Dolmetsch used to build harpsichords. If one admits that it has not been proved that this cannot be done in the electronic world, then those who hear these instruments (or some others from the same firm) may well find it possible to join the many who have been astonished by them.

Since I introduce this firm's name only to make my argument concrete, I hasten to add that I do not know that no other firm can produce work of an equally high quality; I have to say that I have not met it. But there is a limitation within this argument that I must admit at once. The examples of this technique that I admire are either very small or very large. Even this builder is less impressive in the moderate-size range at present. But the fact that he exists causes me to remain agnostic about any judgment concerning the next electronic organ I see. I think this is a view which musicians ought to share, however often in practice their open-mindedness is disappointed.

For the reader's interest I have included, in Appendix II, specifications of what I still believe to be an almost ideal small pipe organ erected in an old building in a confined space, and of the Copeman Hart organ in St. James's, Newcastle upon Tyne.

13

Practical Matters

We turn now to some practical matters whose connection with theology may appear tenuous, but which, taken with some awareness of the principles on which worship is founded, may prove less intractable than they seem to be at present.

It will have become clear that throughout this argument the central practical concern is for the people who are at worship and who are not making musical decisions. But we must not appear to be unconcerned for the musicians themselves.

The Choir and its Director

Residence in the United States has taught me, among many other things, the difference between talking of a choir in a country where the prevailing tradition is Anglican and talking of a choir in one where the Episcopal Church is a minority group. But it was never far from my consciousness that a choir not in a Catholic or Anglican setting is a liturgical anomaly. It is easy, in churches outside those communions, to forget to ask what a choir is, and what an anthem is.

If ancient precedent counts for anything, a choir was originally a body of singers set aside to sing the liturgy, and if they did not sing the liturgy nobody would. Medieval liturgy was not in the modern sense congregational. A monastic choir, which was the archetype, sang daily, usually many times a day. Their music was the sacred routine of the daily round, plus the great climax of high mass on Holy Days. It consisted of men only, and until the late middle ages it sang only plainsong. It was completely different from the celebratory singing group, male and female, conspicuous in position and often in dress, that is dedicated to singing choral music in a large American protestant church.

Under the same dispensation an anthem was a verse or two of a psalm chanted antiphonally during mass to mark the occasion on which mass was sung; it was one of the more important of the variables that altered from one Holy Day to the next. It too was plainsong, sung antiphonally, and "anthem" is a corruption of the older word "antiphon." This again could hardly be more different from a performance of Parry's "I was glad" at a protestant preaching service. There are two references to "anthem" in the old *English Prayer Book* of 1662. One refers to the special chant sung on Easter in place of Psalm 95 (the normal Sunday psalm) as "The Easter Anthems"; this is a compendious piece consisting of verses from various parts of the Pauline Epistles, and it is referred to in the plural because it gave the appearance of being several anthems of the old kind run together (it is much longer than a medieval anthem would have been). The other place is where an anthem is permitted after the third collect at morning and evening prayer, which originally referred to an adoration of the Blessed Virgin, but later, in more puritan times, was simply permitted to be a suitable choral piece.

"Choir" and "anthem" have radically changed their senses since those days. The emergence of congregational singing as a part of worship on the now-familiar scale was a slow process not really taking the shape we know until the advent of the evangelicals. This was a new pattern: choir and congregation instead of, for singing purposes, choir alone. We usually think now that the choir is there to help the congregation and to edify it. Those are two distinct processes. What problems do they raise?

In worship which remains chiefly choral, like the traditional office of sung evensong, there are no problems. Cathedral evensong, where the great English tradition of church music has always been nurtured, is a natural development from the primitive style; the choir carries on conversation with the priest in the course of the service and sings settings of the canticles, and later an anthem, appropriate to its talents. It also, most importantly, sings the psalms, and there is no question that this edifies whatever congregation is present. Not every Christian finds this enlightening, but those whom it does edify, it edifies efficiently. It is contemplative worship, the church's chamber music, and central to its ethos is the principle that it would go on if there were no congregation present at all.

It is in the protestant scene, where "edification" is more narrowly defined to mean instruction through the spoken word, and "participation" is increasingly restricted to mean vocal participation, that the anomalies begin to appear. Protestants should recall, what most of them now forget, that when anthems were first introduced into protestant services—the style being traceable back to those hearty anthem-hymns which the evangelicals invented—everybody present was expected, or at least allowed, to join in. That accounts for the folk-simplicity of their musical style. They were often pieces hardly worth listening to, but serviceable if people of limited musical talent were taking part and nobody was really listening at all. There was in this no breach of the old puritan principle that if any music was made it must be made by all present. It is when people have to listen to a protestant choir that difficulty comes, because we have to determine in what sense they are listening, and what good it does them to listen if they are uninterested in music.

The key to this problem is to discover what common ground there is between the choir and the worshiping people. When we ask the question we find too often that there is plenty of common ground, but that it has been enclosed and made inaccessible by liturgical disorder. Just as one has to say in other places that preaching becomes an exceedingly doubtful form of solo entertainment when it is associated with no kind of prior preparation in the worshiper, so we have to say that choral performances in church are of doubtful value when they take no notice of what the worshiper brings with him to church. But if the church withdraws the supply of what the worshiper could have collected and brought with him, what can we have but confusion? In other words, if the preacher thinks he can get by without consulting the church's year, the choir director certainly cannot. Returning to the ancient principle by which the anthem was the signal telling the worshiper exactly what Sunday it was, we find that it applies exactly in our present case. The secret for protestant churches is, of course, in the lectionary, which gives the text for each Sunday during the year. So as not to ignore altogether those communions or local churches which still do not use a lectionary, the least that the church management can do for the worshiper is to provide him or her well in advance with a schedule of the readings and subjects to be handled at the services for two months ahead.

The responsibility for this rests squarely on the shoulders of the clergy. The idea that no sermon can have spiritual content if it is prepared earlier than Saturday night, and that any planning or worship on this scale diminishes the field of the Holy Spirit's action, is one that should be roundly denounced as egotistic presumptuousness on the part of preachers. It is sacerdotalism of the worst kind to claim that a congregation can contribute anything to worship if one's notion of worship is to present them with perpetual surprises. Surprise is precisely the domain of the Holy Spirit; solid, honest, and disciplined work is the domain of the preacher and it is time he learned it.

This has to be put quite uncompromisingly. Until the discipline of decent neighborliness is accepted by the clergy, until they are content with preaching from Scripture instead of preaching on topics, until they are, moreover, content to be part of the larger community of the church sufficiently to follow a common lectionary, the choirmaster's job remains chaotic and religiously frustrated. It is not enough to encourage choirmasters to make the best of this situation. Making the best of it perpetuates it. No, they should rebel, and insist that the clergy do their work properly. They should be as discontented with the confusion produced by clerical perversity as they have a right to be with their personal stipends; they should even band together in a kind of labor union to get proper working conditions. (The very best thing that the Presbyterians in America got from their *Worshipbook* of 1970 was the lectionary; whatever else in that book may be modified, that must stay.)

116

In any case, the words of an anthem should be placed before the worshiper on paper. This is not to insult the choir's diction. It is to give the unmusical person a visual image of the idea that the choir is setting to music. In any Word-oriented community that is a plain necessity.

I add one suggestion. All Christian churches are impoverished if the psalms are withdrawn from their worship. Very largely in the "family" public worship of the church they have disappeared. This is partly because unless they are metrical psalms (which except in the *American Psalter* of 1912 are usually poor literature) they are difficult to sing congregationally without a good deal of musical organization. The choral singing of psalms is the obvious answer. Let parishes and protestant gatherings learn this from the cathedral tradition. The advantages tumble over each other. Psalms were originally not primarily for congregational singing and many of them are better as solos or choral pieces for people to listen to. Psalms are a precious part of the Bible not provided for in the lectionary of public readings. People still know some of the psalms, and the familiarity of their words will hold their attention. Many psalms are dramatic, having qualities which straight congregational singing misses. Carefully chosen Anglican chants, with changes of chant where the words suggest it, can be very beautiful, and too much attention should not be paid to those who, chiefly in order to promote plainsong, have often said that they are unmusical. There is no more testing discipline for a choir than mastering the subtleties of rhythm which the psalm texts demand; compared with this, the most complicated rhythmic patterns in Byrd or Tippett are child's play. Psalms can, of course, be sung liturgically as a communal reading of the Bible; psalms can be sung as hymns. But above all they make exquisite anthems, and I seriously suggest that in those many places where choral music is required twice in a service one of these occasions be given to the choral singing of a psalm. Since the lectionary usually provides a psalm for the day, the problem of choice is removed. It may be added that nothing is more likely to remove swiftly from a choir any taint of exhibitionism or pomp than the discipline of learning psalmody of this kind.

There is, naturally, everything to be said for a choir's occasionally acting as a free-standing singing body and singing on some occasion music in which musicians will take special delight. The assiduity with which many choirs nowadays do this is commendable. How often one hears of a performance of Haydn's *Nelson Mass* or Fauré's *Requiem*, offered as an enrichment of the church's life, not as a substitute but as a support for worship. In no circumstances should a large-scale musical performance be substituted for worship. There is no such activity as worshiping through music unless one is musical, and the non-musical are short-changed if music deprives them of preaching or the sacraments. But then no church is fully operational whose people never meet for any purpose but worship, and experience has shown that when the church choir, made up after all of friends of the congregation, stages a performance of a major work on some non-worshiping occasion, many people of little musical interest come and find themselves enjoying music more than they thought they would. When that happens, people have indeed been edified and enlarged.

More Decisions for the Organist

I must tread warily in approaching a very controversial point. It concerns the solo pieces played by the organist as a contribution to worship.

Coming into church, the congregation expects to hear the organist playing. Why do they wish this? One of the best answers is that of the late Dr. Nathaniel Micklem, who once said that for non-Catholics the music does what incense does for Catholics—an impact on one of the senses reminds people where they are. Probably for many people the organ voluntary (called in America the prelude) does little more. I become controversial when I say that there is no reason on earth why it should.

I have remarked before on the undoubted fact that America is plentifully supplied with able organ players, far more so than Britain. This is why this is a more acute problem in America. No good artist finds it easy to perform before people who are not listening. The inferior executant is only too relieved that this is so and would be terrified to hear that a trained musician were in the congregation. But facts are facts, and one is that people come to church for nonmusical purposes, and the proper purpose they should have in mind at this point is prayer. It follows that the organist should use modest rather than distracting sounds before the service. The most acute point of controversy comes when I venture to advise that this means predominantly quiet sounds.

A fine organist delights in great organ music, and great organ music often rises to a massive climax near the end. What happens then is that while most people are saying their prayers, a deafening sound comes from the instrument (and I am afraid that's all it means to quite a number of people—a deafening sound distracting from their prayers). Remember, prayers are unspoken words; it's difficult to hear the words forming in your mind when a loud sound is assailing your ears, no matter how majestic the music. The result can be complaints if people are taking their worship seriously, and these always surprise and dismay the player who was sincerely offering great music because it never occurred to him to ask whether this wasn't a present costly but misplaced.

The music can distract, of course, without being noisy. A very well-known melody is probably less useful than something which the ordinary listener receives as simply a sound pattern. The chorale preludes of J. S. Bach are ideal for this purpose simply because people (if they are not Lutherans) don't usually know the tunes they are based on and, in any case, Bach makes them delightfully unrecognizable. Abstract rather than ear-catching music is, at this point, the most welcome kind.

But many congregations make the organist's work more frustrating than it need be by treating his or her music as Muzak, a background to conversation. It cannot (I think) be emphasized too much how unneighborly, thoughtless, and self-indulgent is the behavior of those who gossip in the sanctuary whether before or after the service. This is enough to make the organist play loudly in order to drown the chatter, but the louder the organ sound, the louder the conversation. To this abuse (which should not be taken as a reason for overlooking the principle we have just drawn attention to) there is only one answer, and it will serve also to make it easier for the organist at the end of the service, where a festive sound is always appropriate. This is to instruct the congregation firmly and courteously that conversation, except on matters directly affecting the duties of those who administer the church's life, is out of place before and after the service. Nowhere is this done more kindly and more convincingly than at Coventry Cathedral, England, where the congregation can read in a small and beautiful explanatory handbook not only what evensong is but also this instruction: "Before you leave—do not be in a hurry to go—pray for us; and do nothing to disturb those who wish to hear the music played on the organ." That is an injunction which could well be printed in church bulletins.

It will have been noticed how many of the judgments we are making revolve round neighborliness and tolerable manners. The horror of any kind of silence is a frequent symptom in Britain; in some American circles it is a disease in an advanced stage. Choirs and clergy chatter about everything under the sun until seconds before the service, and naturally congregations follow their example. It is considered unneighborly *not* to chatter. The truth that it is at some seasons unneighborly to chatter is always overlooked. In extreme cases there is only one remedy. This is to ask the organist to collaborate by keeping the instrument silent altogether before the introit or the first hymn; then to instruct the choir, after the vestry prayer, to remain totally silent until they open their mouths in song; then for the clergy to take on themselves a two-minute Trappist vow—and only when everybody has got used to silence (the removal of the organ music for a while is the best way of shutting up the gossipers; they soon feel out of place) should the pre-service voluntary be restored.

One other well-intentioned error is that of using devices to keep the congregation as a captive audience for the music before and after service. Except on occasions when only musicians are present (for example in a music-college chapel or at a conference) this should never be done. It will only engender in the well-meaning unmusical perverse and heathen ideas about worshiping through music, or will, alternatively, bore them. It is a confusion of categories to do in church what is only appropriate to a strictly musical occasion.

As to the use of other instruments in addition to or instead of the organ for music before or after the service, provided the principles above are observed and the instruments are as nearly as possible impeccably played, they provide a most refreshing enrichment and should be encouraged. But the soloist should be as nearly invisible as is compatible with audibility, and the soloist should on no account be a singer; singing at a service should be kept for the liturgy.

The Organist and the Congregation

Finally let us return to the organist's duty and delight—the encouraging of music out of an unmusical congregation. Several points often emerge when I am involved in discussion of these matters and brief treatments of them can be included here. We are taking up the tale of hymn playing where we dropped it in the previous chapter, and will first deal with the speed at which hymns should be played.

There is no hard and fast rule about this, and musicianship—especially some knowledge of what sort of musical tradition the hymn tune comes from—should be a sufficient guide. Vaughan Williams in the *English Hymnal* had what almost amounted to a mania for slowness, which caused him to insert metronome marks against every tune; he marks the Bach version of EIN' FESTE BURG ("A mighty fortress") at m.m. 40, which means that the four stanzas of that hymn would take rather longer to sing than the first movement of Beethoven's Pathétique Sonata takes to play, with repeats. Even his own "For all the saints" is marked at 112. It is common knowledge that American organists play hymns faster than the English, probably because American buildings are almost always less acoustically lively than English ones. If excessive slowness suggests pomp, excessive speed undoubtedly suggests hustle. And nothing could be less musicianly than to play all tunes at the same speed—the

PASSION CHORALE, to take an extreme example, at the same speed as AURELIA ("The church's one foundation") which is in the same meter. Musicians usually feel, if they give any thought to it, that a musically trivial tune needs to be rescued by a gentler tempo than some great tunes; certainly tunes containing many examples of more than one note to a syllable should never be hurried. It is important to remember that one can use a slow tempo and still impart energy through phrasing and strong rhythm. But there is no overall answer to the question "How fast should hymns go?" It depends on the hymn, the size of the congregation, the acoustics of the building, and not least, the weather.

Unison, Harmony, and Pitch

This at once brings us to the question whether congregations should sing in unison or in harmony. Here opinions divide. Most English musicians follow Dr. Vaughan Williams in preferring that the congregation sing in unison. But in Wales harmony is insisted on, and American hymnals suggest that it is also expected there. In English congregations, and in almost all English choirs, the men prefer harmony because the melody often goes outside their range (for the average English male voice is a bass-baritone) and because they feel it beneath their dignity to sing what the women or boys are singing.

The chief advantage of unison singing is that it is agreeable to a fairly quick tempo, whereas the languor encouraged by part-singing, especially when it is not professionally done, is an inhibition to true Christian zeal. (This point is, of course, not made by Vaughan Williams in the English Hymnal, which prefers unison singing plus slow singing.)

In a famous passage Dietrich Bonhoeffer wrote this about unison singing:

> Because it is bound wholly to the Word, the singing of the congregation, especially of the family congregation, is essentially singing in unison. Here words and music combine in a unique way. . . . The purity of unison singing, unaffected by alien motives of musical techniques, the clarity, unspoiled by

122

the attempt to give musical art an autonomy of its own apart from the words, the simplicity and frugality, the humaneness and warmth of this way of singing is the essence of all congregational singing. . . . It becomes a question of a congregation's power of spiritual discernment whether it adopts unison singing.[1]

There are several reasons why I believe that people in the English tradition should hesitate to take uncritically the advice of German authorities on musical matters. For one thing, the contempt of the typical modern German-speaking Lutheran and reformed pastor for any kind of organistic style or expression in playing hymns, and the manner in which this precept is sometimes expressed, leave the impression that in the presence of high-church Lutherans or reformed authorities music is very much a paid servant. I also find in certain phrases of Bonhoeffer (and in the German-based regions of the United States) a tendency to come down rather hard against any sign of musical autonomy. I believe this to be less than neighborly and less than wise. However, we may learn something from Bonhoeffer's underlying contention, which is that the objections to unison singing in church are more temperamental than theological when voiced by the singers—too high for men, too low for women, none of them able to use their best notes, not so *interesting* as part-singing.

This is the sort of thing about which St. Paul would have said, "I have no instructions from the Lord." There are principles, but not regulations. Some music is written in a unison texture, some in a four-part texture, and there are no rules which forbid either for use in church. On the one hand, S. S. Wesley's tune HEREFORD[2] is surely beautiful and would be murdered by being sung unison in D major. On the other hand, a fast-moving tune with a slower bass might become stodgy if attempted in parts (my own tune, WANSBECK,[3] is an example of a tune written in unison so as to allow the bass to move at a different rate from the melody). It is true that a few

[1]Dietrich Bonhoeffer, *Life Together* (SCM, 1954), p. 50.
[2]H-1940, Number 463.
[3]*Ecumenical Praise*, Number 87.

tunes we are accustomed to singing in harmony are often improved by being translated into unison texture. Among these are the old psalm tunes (which are essentially unison melodies) and some of the stronger Victorian tunes. One thinks of the especially good effect of Goss's unison first and last verses in "Praise, my soul," and how much this tune loses when printed, as always in America, with the harmony version alone.

Another example is Barnby's pleasant tune to "When morning gilds the skies," which seems to gain a good deal from being transposed slightly down, scored for unison singing, and marked "fast."[4] Two more examples follow which indicate how a psalm tune could be treated, and how another Barnby tune, slightly sticky in the SATB version, can be enlivened by moving the bass more slowly than the melody (which can now go fast).

[4]*Hymns for Church and School,* Number 230.

124

I personally lean toward the unison texture, and it is certainly true that most modern composers, wanting a lighter and more flexible form of melody than used to be in vogue, use it constantly. The freedom from stodgy singing is the reason they use it. Therefore, if some musicians have felt that sufficient concessions have already been demanded from them in favor of congregations in these pages, I here ask that congregations be encouraged to offer a little cooperation. Congregational singers are often lazy or apathetic and need encouragement. Most modern editors accept the D-D norm for a tune written within the octave, only going beyond it at the top if they are also obliged to go beyond it at the bottom. There will, of course, be some who find even this a strain because of old age, sinus trouble, or an unusually deep voice; but the advantage of accommodating them has to be set against the undoubted disadvantage of pitching tunes so low that while it is easy for everybody to sing carelessly (except the occasional tenor who will have to move up to the alto line) the total effect will be one of settled gloom. However, an organist worth his or her salt will be able to play a tune in any key at sight, and now and again transposition may be advisable. It is entirely up to the organist to decide.

Modulation, Interlude, and Varied Harmony

The only evidence we usually get of an organist's being able to transpose, however, is in the curious custom which prevails here and there of playing a final stanza half a tone or a whole tone higher than the rest of the hymn. This is done by people so respectable and distinguished that it will seem over-bold if I state my own view, which is that this is a wholly unmusical thing to do. I believe it to be a spillover from the trivial music of the pop culture, in which a tonal hitch-up is very frequent at a repetition of a melody. If you do this you are thinking of the hymn as three, four, or five musical units, and that is a deadly way to approach a hymn. Its text is a single unit, so its music must be.

Modulation often follows an interlude which is used as a run-up to the final stanza. The interlude can be used to point a climax, or to lengthen a hymn which turns out to be too short to cover some other activity. In either case the interlude can be very effective if it is done in a musicianly way; a very severe degree of self-criciticm must be built into any organist who attempts to do it without preparation. The use of an interlude to lengthen a hymn which turns out to be too short leads me to suggest that on those occasions, which should be rare, when a hymn accompanies a procession, it is better to choose a longer hymn and time the procession properly than to leave the organist stranded with the necessity of improvising fillers between stanzas.

I am here reminded of the need to say that processional hymns are properly used to mark special days of celebration, and that there is no conceivable justification for beginning every service with one. In fact, except on Palm Sunday, processional hymns do not belong at the beginning of the service at all. The widespread belief that the choir cannot be decently got into the church unless the congregation, whom they are supposed to help sing, is struggling around them with a hymn while they struggle up the nave to the chancel is as ill-founded as the belief that an amen should follow every hymn. This practice is a product of that insecure pompousness which has accompanied liturgical uncertainty. The choir should either enter in silence while the organist plays, or enter singing without asking the congregation to sing with them. That last practice is difficult but effective and revives the true introit or Entrance Song. Once the choir is in place, the opening call to praise should be said by the minister (I here presuppose a protestant service) and praise should then be offered by all present. No gesture (of which this opening procession and closing recession are bothersome examples) should be made which suggests that the choir is not part of the worshiping congregation; nor should the clergy enter separately from the choir, implying that the choir is not also part of the appointed ministry of the church.

We are now left with the practice of varying accompaniments, which is, I find, more common in Britain than in America. This brings out the fact that American organists are, by training if not by temperament, more efficient and technically able than their English counterparts, but less likely to regard playing as a creative activity; or, if preferred, that English organists practice less but invent more. The virtues and vices of the two kinds of player are complementary but different. Playing hymns is an activity in which we might welcome more precision than some of the English provide, but much more indication of personal interest in the music than some of the Americans provide.

These things are required if one proposes to vary harmonies: (1) an indication that all present must sing that stanza in unison (provided in many English hymn books but never in the United States); (2) careful preparation by the organist; (3) a version which is in a style current with or earlier than, but not after, the hymn tune; (4) the unmusical member of the congregation should react not by feeling he was interfered with, nor by feeling how clever the organist was, but by saying that that particular hymn went unusually well.

Many volumes of varied accompaniments are available. While I give a list of these in Appendix I, I do not feel that any are wholly satisfactory, and tend to feel that an able organist can just as well devise his or her own comment on a good tune. My objection to most books of variations is that they seem mostly to ignore the third point above, which to a musician ought to be of the greatest importance. In practice this is not a very onerous restriction, since the whole of the musical vocabulary we shall be likely to want to use was settled by the time Bach died, so it is only tunes written before 1750 which demand special care here. But even so, one should take reasonable care to write a varied version so that it reflects the spirit of the tune, and to reserve chromaticism for the more reflective and penitential tunes, as Bach did.

Not to let this degenerate into a technical treatise, I

simply offer three hints to those who attempt this often very fruitful and inspiring exercise. First, if the arrangement is fully composed with a totally independent organ part, make such use as you can of important musical figures in the melody. Second, see that the bass (with which one should always begin) remains in good counterpoint with the melody; and third, make as much use as possible of scales, diatonic or chromatic, which always produces a well-engineered piece. I also offer in Appendix I some fragments and complete harmonizations to indicate certain styles in which this can be done without musical offense.

The Choirmaster

Another large difference between normal practice in America and in Britain is the dividing of the offices of organist and choirmaster, or music director. The reflections of one to whom this is strange may or may not interest those for whom it is normal, but I offer these.

The chief reflection is what a vast difference it makes to music-making when the business becomes not a Duo but a Trinity,—Director, Organist, Choir. It is a situation which in England one associates normally with very large and special occasions where a choir is so big as to need a conductor or where the virtuoso reputation of the choir (as in King's, Cambridge and some cathedrals) stands so high that a con ductor is required almost all the time in the choir stalls. It is not there a normal parish situation, and indeed plenty of respectable English and Scottish choirs are so sited that their organist cannot without considerable difficulty conduct from the console. In England I have often felt that when a choir is singing an anthem, and is an amateur body that needs constant reassurance, the scruples about conducting in church are misplaced, and an assistant organist accompanying while the Director conducted would give a far better and more assured performance. But obviously this is not necessary in hymns.

The thing that needs watching is something of which few are conscious but which has an effect whose further consequences we have already noticed. This is that the over-all authority, the Director, is not the person who produces the sound. The organist is in this collaboration the junior partner. Now the organist may be a national celebrity as a recitalist, but he or she is in church under the authority of the Director, and therefore an accompanist. It may be that in Britain we get (or can get) more expressive playing of hymns simply because the player of a hymn for a congregation has to exert an authority directly over the congregation which the church organist in the American situation never realizes he or she ought to exert. Accompanying other musicians is one kind of activity: accompanying a congregation is another, to which one must bring imagination, initiative, and a capacity for giving a lead which comes through to the congregation as reassurance. Playing for the choir, you are watching and listening, or if you are on your own, listening simply for what they are singing. Playing for a congregation you are listening for all manner of other things including how they are feeling and whether they are getting hold of the tune. I have never yet heard in America what happens when a congregation has to be assisted through a not very familiar hymn simply by the sounds from the organ, but I am familiar enough with the phenomenon in Britain, and only a few weeks before writing these lines witnessed what happened when a really skilled veteran at a large organ in a famous Scottish church had to help through an unknown hymn a congregation that knew it tolerably well and an accomplished American visiting choir who had never seen it at all. This can only be done by somebody who is up to all manner of tricks for making people feel at home with music. I more than half suspect that the terror of unfamiliar hymns in America, and the relative lack of interest in hymns at all on the part of organists is traceable to the fact that this particular kind of organistic initiative is atrophied by the presence of a Director who is not playing. All that is needed is that the Director shall be interested in hymns and encourage these skills, which are thirty per cent pastoral after all, in the organist.

But the choir director has great responsibilities anyhow, and upon his discharge of them a great deal else rests. The last thing I would ask for is the abolition of the director and the copying in America of what Britain does. On the con-

129

trary, the Director is often an assistant minister so far as his flock are concerned; he often has time to be contemplative about the inwardness of his responsibility that an organist, especially a young one, has not. He (or she) it is who should always set the example of liturgical sensitiveness. He it is who must lead the rebellion I asked for earlier. He it is who must be familiar with the liturgy and the lectionary, the chief interpreter in music of the mysteries otherwise committed to the clergy. The position of Music Director or, as some say, Minister of Music, is an exalted one; indeed the very existence on some churches of the title, Minister of Music, suggests the most promising path towards those reconciliations between theology and music to which much earlier we referred.

But we have stumbled on a new point here which must lead us towards our conclusion.

14

Musicians, Music, and Church Order

The late C. S. Lewis, when persuaded to set down his thoughts about church music, wrote one of his most ill-tempered articles, in which he said that church music was useful as a necessary discipline whose unpleasantness was probably good for the souls that endured it, but that if it were ever made in the spirit of offering God a gift, it would likely be positively harmful to all concerned.[1]

No church musician ought to be shielded from the thought that there are in any congregation not only a number of unmusical people but also a smaller number who positively dislike church music. They are always a minority, but they do us a great service by being there. They call a necessary halt to starry-eyed notions that music is a great unifier, or that through music everybody is assisted in worship. "Worship without music," wrote the Precentor of Coventry in his booklet *Evensong at Coventry Cathedral*, "does not easily soar." For most people that is true; but for a few it has the opposite reaction.

C. S. Lewis had his own reasons for disliking church music, but never explained them. He especially disliked hymns, and never spoke of congregations singing them; the verb he used was "shouting." Now that we know so much of this extraordinary man, my conjecture is that in singing hymns the church presented itself to him as either complacently self-admiring (in choral music) or as a gang or an "inner ring" (in hymns). His was a temperament to which protestant churches are especially inhospitable—contemplative and individualistic and disinclined for the religious life-style known as "getting involved"; he was especially sensitive to deliberately exclusive cliques, a reaction

---

[1]C. S. Lewis, *Christian Reflections* (Grand Rapids, Michigan: Eerdmans, 1971), pp. 94ff.

attributable to his disagreeable experiences at school. The church was to him a place of quietness in which he could at leisure and with awe contemplate the mysteries of his faith; the early morning service without music pleased him most.

In the second book I ever wrote about hymns I wrote on its opening page of my own consciousness to what an extent the music of the church, especially hymnody, was repellent to those outside it; and although this is no place to offer personal advertisement of any sort, I could truthfully say that all the unpleasant experiences associated with the church in my own early childhood were centered on its music. (I can distinctly remember as an infant being caused to howl by the sound of an organ, and as a small child, before the age of eight, being actively repelled by the sound of the church choir I used often to hear.)

This brings me to the last point—the danger of *divisiveness* in church music. It is a danger mostly hidden from musicians because music is, in so many ways, a unifying factor in the church. Music has always flowed freely like floodwater over denominational frontiers. Even if sturdy nonconformists were unwilling to have anything to do with Anglicans, they sang "Holy, holy, holy" without discomfort; Roman Catholics before 1964 were content to use tunes by non-Catholic composers when original texts by non-Catholic authors were forbidden. In other familiar ways also, music has brought people together who would not have been likely to meet, through choral societies or large interdenominational singing festivals. However, this refers to the unification of people who enjoy music, or at least enjoy singing. The generation of corporate emotion and religious zeal which is familiar in any large crowd gathered for religious purposes, whether it is a Billy Graham rally or a diocesan music festival, can easily appear to the participants to be the whole of religious experience; they can come easily to feel that any who do not participate are dissenters whom they have a right to despise or pity. The strange indignation which accompanies enthusiastic praise of great gatherings, "I can't understand how people can stay away," betokens a mind closed to the needs of the contemplative worshiper who refuses to be brainwashed by music, good or bad. Such a worshiper is not a hermit; he does not reject the community of the church. He only asks that it be a little less talkative, and that he be listened to.

Wherever church music of any kind is associated with operations that bear the marks of what this world calls success (which crudely means exerting an appeal to large numbers of people), a touch of suspicion should creep in. It is much more important to say this than to spend time criticizing the semi-civilized music that often accompanies so-called religious revivals. I believe that if an operation is associated with barbarous music, it will not be a true religious revival at all. But I go along with Lewis in warning my reader that that proposition is not reversible—to have first-class music does not guarantee that the religion thus "revived" is true religion. There is certainly a case for saying that the immense gatherings of the Kirchentag movement in Germany in the years immediately following the First World War were a greater contribution to the refreshment of religion than most large American evangelistic rallies or television revivals are. The superiority of Kirchentag music to gospel songs or the so-called modern religious folk style is not unconnected with the more alert theology offered by the preachers in that movement—but this is not wholly safe ground to stand or build on.

C. S. Lewis was probably a member of a fairly small minority, though that minority should never be overlooked in the church. It happens that our own age, increasingly so since Lewis's time, is an age of clamorous and rancid divisions. There is a special temptation deliberately to do divisive things in the church; theology which rejects well-worn doctrines always sells better than that which refreshes and revives them. I always held that Honest to God (1963) was popular for the wrong reasons, and a regular series of utterances in theology since then has been promoted by enterprising publishers. They do little harm, perhaps some good, if confined to the learned and alert, but in fact they get into the hands of people whose faith they simply erode and diminish. Similarly, the media tend to emphasize points of division like the generation gap, the race gap, the South/North axis in the United States, and the class war in Britain.

133

Consequently, on the one hand people are more sensitive than they were to the tendency to favor one interest at the expense of another; on the other hand, people are more ready to draw attention to themselves by emphasizing and fomenting these divisions.

Church music has not been unaffected by all this. The music scene since the early 1950s has been the exact reflection of a religious scene in which the irenic and accepting mind has been held in contempt, and the aggressive and rejecting mind celebrated. We now have the shocking spectacle of churches feeling obliged to run two services on a Sunday morning, one popular or modern, the other traditional, thus effectively dividing their congregations into two parties which find it convenient not to meet.[2] We have seen, correspondingly, a division in music between the trend-seekers and the traditionals. Innovation rudely defied development. The Twentieth Century Church Light Music Group in England was the first group to make this gesture in Britain. History seems to insist that there has been no other point at which such a clean break with tradition was made as was made there, except possibly at the English Restoration. The fact that it was so largely a clerical movement increased

[2]I hope it will not be taken too much as a "sour grapes" comment by an Englishman if I state my opinion that the now very common practice in America of offering at least two services on Sunday morning which are exactly alike is not without its theological difficulties. The normal reason for doing this is that a church building cannot accommodate all who want to attend if they all want to come at once. But what happens is that family A opts for the earlier service, family B for the later, and they are likely never to meet. True, the interval between the services is often used for excellent educational programs or even more excellent social gatherings at which family A could meet family B if it wanted, and this is good. But when one belongs to a Christian community and never sees that community fully assembled, surely something is lost. It is now economically irreversible, of course; but the alternative, when a church building is full to overflowing, might have been to open another in a different area. A sanctuary seating 800 can happily accommodate a membership of at least 1,200. Memberships exceeding 2,000 begin to look as if they would be better employed staffing several churches. Those exceeding 10,000 (a few still exist) seem totally unintelligible. But implementing this would, of course, have involved a radically different view of the ministry and of lay responsibility from that which prevailed when these customs began. There would also have to have been a great deal of "tentmaking" among ministers and a strenuous sense of stewardship to maintain several small churches instead of one enormous one. Nonetheless, we lost something when this came about.

its effectiveness in initiating the demolition of the church as people knew it; it was an overt statement that the church largely needed demolishing. Sydney Carter's folk songs, often so penetrating, some almost prophetic in their interpretation of the restlessness of the British Christian mind, contributed to this cause in their frequent insistence on the inadequacy and dispensableness of the church. The cause has been gleefully taken up by the popular composers of the United States and has been very largely associated, without their permission, with the young of this generation. Ninety percent of the mythology that all this has generated is false, artificial, and malicious.

The activism, protest, divisiveness, and downright malice which paraded themselves in one new popular love song after another has had a calamitous effect on Roman Catholic devotion. The musician has to ask of his music "Whom is this leaving out?" and he will find that it isn't just the nonmusical, but whole groups of people. Factions, parties, and trends have brought *odium theologicum* into the market place and this is advertised as being a very healthy situation. The educated laity in the churches becomes strident, the committed people moralistic, the reformers pharisaic, and the person who simply wants to get refreshment and nourishment from the church is about the last person who is considered. Compared with theologians, church musicians are peaceable people. Compared with the present theological scene the church music scene is placid. Indeed I am seeing a good deal more sanity in the mainstream of church music than I detect in the theology that comes my way. But there is no use in complaining without attempting a diagnosis and, if not a cure, a plan of resistance.

There are now, it seems to me, several kinds of divisive music. The one to which I have referred seems malignant. The second kind of divisiveness occurs when a religious group pursues any music tradition to the exclusion of others. My criticism of the gospel song tradition, until recently so exclusively cultivated by the Southern Baptists but to some extent respected in many other American groups, is that it is dissuasive to growth and maturity; it is too undemanding, too likely, in words and music which conform so closely to a single style, to restrict a believer's view of his faith to a very narrow compass. It is not its familiarity but the restriction of its subject matter that prompts this comment. I am equally cautious about any group which sings nothing but Genevan psalms, classic German chorales, or folk music. The glory of church music, now that in our century the whole treasury has been made available to all, is its diversity. A service can contain the "Old Hundredth," "Ye Holy Angels Bright," and "For All the Saints," and bring, by way of utterly familiar texts and music, six cultures into one act of worship (the Genevan, the Scottish and English, the puritan, the Handelian eighteenth century, the Victorian, and the early twentieth century). A church blessed with such diversity of heritage should welcome a diversity of people. One that is exclusively high church or low church in its musical appointments is one that will be fastidious about the kind of people it will accept in friendship.

Another kind of music which presents problems is ethnic music. The presence on the general scene now (it appears only recently in general hymnals) of the black spiritual reminds us that in a sense all western music is ethnic and that the ecumenical movement is still only in its infancy. The maturity of western music is expressed in its diversity, but even so, western ears have not yet done much with Chinese or far eastern traditional music. How clear it is that the use of ethnic music can be either ecumenical or divisive, depending on the spirit in which it is used! Black spirituals should be used by white people with alertness and caution, with some knowledge of what kind of worship and culture they were composed for, and with no trace of ecumenical pomposity or patronage. (The thing to note especially is that they are not narrative or affirmative, like other western hymns, but dramatic and ecstatic.) We must be aware that in this day there are those who would corrupt a sincere and innocent desire to widen frontiers, bridge gaps, and enlarge sympathies. This is the peculiar weakness and grief of our age.

What then should the church musician be doing? The only answer is to exorcize as far as possible divisive attitudes and thoughts, and to celebrate that which is really the common music of as many kinds of people as possible. This is

136

not pop or trendy music; it is not ephemeral, posturing music. It is precisely the "Old Hundredth," "Ye Holy Angels Bright" and "For All the Saints"—nobody need claim to be too cultured to respect those, and nobody does claim to be too uneducated to enjoy them. In choral and organ music the trained musician knows where to find authenticity whether it is English Anglican, German baroque, verse-anthem, Howells, Britten, or the fine clear stream that is flowing through modern American music. The musician must not yield to pressure and set aside his knowledge and the conscience and discernment he or she has developed. Blessed, remember, are not the peace lovers, but the peacemakers.

Congregations are waiting for, and ready to respond to, those who will offer them in contemporary language the eternal truths of the faith and the unchanging moralities agreed on by all the great civilizations of the world. They are waiting for a reconciling and accepting music which will nourish their Christian growth. It always was available; people have not stopped writing it despite the blandishments of those who offer them rich rewards for writing otherwise. It is still true that the Church is the preserver and refiner of sanity. There is still something against which the gates of hell will not prevail.

In conclusion, the theological judgments on musical decision that I am pleading for are secondary to the greater concern of service to the church whose existence is in and through Jesus Christ. It is, I trust, no pietist platitude to claim that our music and our music making should aim at being conformable to a gospel which tells of a crucified and risen Redeemer, and which lays on us all the duty and the delight of losing our lives that we may save them.

I am not pessimistic but impatient. My impatience is that of a schoolboy who wants the time to pass quickly before the holidays come. I sense the brightness of the promises. It might look as if I see my neighbors' practices and efforts in dark colors. I do not. There has been progress, and there never were more lively signs of hope. It is the good student upon whom the teacher lays the toughest burdens and whom the teacher criticizes most ruthlessly.

One final word. In earlier days I used to ask why the

churches never provided in their books of discipline and order any ceremony for the recognition of church musicians comparable to that for the ordination of elders. I do not ask that question now. I ask for the temporal and economic recognition of musicians and their work, and I object as much as ever to musicians being wholly in the power of people who neither have nor seek any understanding of musicians' problems. But I do not now ask for ordination ceremonies. (I believe that in some churches where the title minister of music is used they actually have them, and I am not sure that it has done much good.) The mistake I made is that mistake one would make in asking for the recognition of people who build churches or make stained-glass windows for cathedrals.

Leave that as it is; it is better so. A musician is an artist employed by the church who hopes to be able to give what he or she has for the edifying of the church's people. To lay hands on the musician in ordination would be not only anomalous; it would probably become an excuse for doing no more. No, don't lay hands on the musicians. Talk to them.

Appendix I

Bibliography of Varied Organ Accompaniments

Bairstow, Edward. *Organ Accompaniments* to the Unison
Verses of 24 Hymn Tunes from the English Hymnal.
Oxford University Press, 1941.
Musicianly and organistically exciting in a style typical of
the period. Less austere than that recommended in this
book but often interesting, and often providing more than
one setting for a tune.

Dickinson, Peter. *Hymn Tunes Made New.* Novello, 1964.
This will appeal to those who think the advice given in
this book misguided and who enjoy fierce and alarming
discords. It includes 22 tunes.

Hancock, Gerre. *Organ Improvisations for Hymn Singing.*
Hinshaw Music, 1975.
Forty-eight tunes varied by one of the most accomplished
hymn-accompanists of the present generation in the
United States.

Knight, G. H., ed. *Accompaniments for Unison Hymn Singing.* England: The Royal School of Church Music, un-
dated, about 1972.
Fifty varied harmonies by different composers. A mixed
bag.

Thiman, Eric H. *Varied Harmonies to Hymn Tunes.* Oxford
University Press, 1934.
A short practical treatise.

Fragments and Examples (see pages 127 and 128)

This fragment is intolerable, I think; the musicians of
1551 didn't use that langauge.

The following is possible. It owes a certain amount to Vaughan Williams, inevitably:

Possible. The unremitting chromatic descent has something to be said for it, but the resulting harmonies contain certain incongruous moments.

The following might be better, since it contains much more diatonic harmony. Beware, however, of introducing a flattened seventh in the last chord but one.

Chromaticism is not incongruous here because the tune WALSALL is very contemplative and is likely to be set to a text containing plenty of pathos, like "Alas, and did my Savior bleed?"

But contrast the diatonic scale in this verse of the hymn "All Creatures," which usually goes to the very openhearted tune LASST UNS ERFREUEN:

Here is an extremely effective example of "one-chord" reharmonization, heard in Salisbury Cathedral, England, in 1950. Note the surprise effect of the "false relation." Only the marked chord alters the harmony of the original (NATIVITY; *English Hymnal*, Number 376).

The tune THORNBURY, very well known in Britain, ends every stanza with a tonic pedal in its last two measures, and indeed it has no V-I bass progression anywhere, which gives it something of the effect of a sentence without a main verb. Delaying the final cadence in the following fashion, in the last stanza, kills two birds with one stone.

A "contrary motion" ending for Darwall's 148th:

Appendix II

Two manuals and pedals.

Swell Organ

1	Double gedeckt (to tenor C)	16
2	Gedeckt	8
3	Spitzflote	8
4	Gedeckt octave	4
5	Spitz octave	4
6	Gedeckt Twelfth	2 2/3
7	Gedeckt Superoctave	2
8	Spitz superoctave	2
9	Spitz 22nd	I
10	Sesquialtera (12, 17)	II
11	Sesquialtera (19, 24)	II
12	Cromhorne	16
13	Cromhorne octave	8
	Tremulant	

Great organ

14	Open Diapason	8
15	Stopped Diapason	8
16	Dulciana	8
17	Principal	4
18	Rohrflote	4
19	Fifteenth	2
20	Mixture (19, 22, 26)	III

Pedal organ

21	Bourdon	16
22	Quint	10 2/3

23 Principal	8
24 Flote	8
25 Fifteenth	4
26 Octave Flote	4
27 Superoctave	2
28 Cromhorne	16
29 Cromhorne octave	8

Couplers: Swell-Great, Swell-Pedal, Great-Pedal: Great
and Pedal Combinations

Accessories: Four pistons to each department
Reversible pistons, Swell-Great and Great-Pedal couplers
Balanced Swell pedal
Double touch cancel on stop keys

The organ was built in 1953 by J. W. Walker & Son of
Ruislip, in consultation with the organist, Mr. John Webster. The Swell organ is built from three ranks of pipes (Gedeckt, Spitz, and Cromhorne) plus the sesquialtera, and occupies a very small space. A descriptive article on this organ
will be found in *The Organ*, (April, 1958), pp. 191ff.

*Specification of the Organ in St. James's Church, Newcastle
upon Tyne*

St. James's Church (United Reformed) is located on
Northumberland Road in Newcastle upon Tyne, England.
The organ was built by Copeman Hart in 1973.

Manual compass CC to C, 61 notes; Pedal CCC to G, 32
notes. There are 84 speaking stops and 16 couplers etc.,
making a total of 100 drawstops.

Great Organ	
1 Double Diapason	16
2 Open Diapason I	8
3 Open Diapason II	8
4 Hohl Flute	8
5 Octave	4

6 Principal	4
7 Harmonic Flute	4
8 Quint	5 1/3
9 Twelfth	2 2/3
10 Fifteenth	2
11 Fourniture	IV
12 Scharf	III
13 Bass Trumpet	16
14 Trumpet	8
15 Clarion	4

Swell Organ

16 Open Diapason	8
17 Stopped Diapason	8
18 Salicional	8
19 Voix Celestes	8
20 Octave	4
21 Rohr Flote	4
22 Nazard	2 2/3
23 Fifteenth	2
24 Flautina	2
25 Mixture	IV
26 Double Trumpet	16
27 Trumpet	8
28 Oboe	8
29 Clarion	4

Positive Organ

30 Nason Flute	8
31 Gedeckt	8
32 Principal	4
33 Flute	4
34 Nazard	2 2/3
35 Octave	2
36 Blockflote	2
37 Tierce	1 3/5
38 Larigot	1 1/3
39 Sifflote	1

40 None	8/9
41 Cymbale	IV
42 Acuta	III
43 Rohr Schalmei	16
44 Cromorne	8

Solo Organ

45 Bass Viol	16
46 Gamba	8
47 Claribel Flute	8
48 Chimney Flute	8
49 Vox Angelica	8
50 Unda Maris	8
51 Octave Gamba	4
52 Koppel Flute	4
53 Twelfth	2 2/3
54 Sylvestrina	2
55 Piccolo	2
56 Mixture	IV
57 Cornet	IV
Tremulant	
58 Tuba	8
59 Trompeta Real	8
60 Clarinet	8
61 Orchestral Oboe	8

Pedal Organ

62 Double Open Wood	32
63 Contra Violone	32
64 Open Wood	16
65 Principal	16
66 Violone	16
67 Bourdon	16
68 Echo Bourdon	16
69 Octave	8
70 Principal	8
71 Bass Flute	8
72 Twelfth	5 1/3

73 Fifteenth	4
74 Octave Flute	4
75 Mixture	V
76 Bombarde	32
77 Contra Posaune	32
78 Ophicleide	16
79 Fagotto	16
80 Rohr Schalmei	16
81 Posaune	8
82 Cromorne	8
83 Clarion	4
84 Schalmei	4

Couplers

Positive to Pedal
Great to Pedal
Swell to Pedal
Solo to Pedal
Swell to Positive
Solo to Positive
Positive to Great
Swell to Great
Solo to Great
Solo to Swell
Swell Octave
Swell Sub Octave
Solo Octave
Solo Sub Octave

Accessories:
Six thumb pistons to Positive
Eight thumb pistons to Great (duplicating Pedal on second touch)
Six thumb pistons to Swell
Six thumb pistons to Solo
Eight toe pistons to Pedal
Reversible thumb piston for Great to Pedal
Reversible toe piston for Great to Pedal
Reversible thumb piston Positive to Pedal

Reversible thumb piston Swell to Pedal
Reversible thumb piston Solo to Pedal
Reversible toe piston Solo to Pedal
Reversible thumb piston Swell to Great
Reversible toe piston Swell to Great
Reversible thumb piston Positive to Great
Reversible thumb piston Solo to Great
Reversible thumb piston pp
Reversible toe piston pp
Reversible thumb piston ff
Reversible toe piston ff
Drawstop console; speaking stops lettered in black; couplers, etc. in red
Simulated tracker action
Balanced Solo pedal
Balanced Swell pedal
Balanced Positive pedal
On/Off button switch
All pistons adjustable at console

Bibliography

Allt, Greenhouse. Lecture to the International Association of Organists, reprinted by M. Hinrichsen, ed., *Organ and Choral Aspects and Prospects*. Hinrichsen, 1958.

Aquinas, St. Thomas. *Summa Theologica*. Ia IIae xxvii I.

Archbishop's Committee's Report, *Music in Church*. SPCK, 1951.

Augustine. *De Vera Religione* 4.

Barton, J. E. *Purpose and Admiration*. Christophers, 1932.

Blake, Leonard, Ed. *English Church Music*. Vol. 27, no. 3.

Bonhoeffer, Dietrich. *Life Together*, English translation. SCM, 1954.

Brown, R. E. C. *The Ministry of the Word*. SCM Press, 1954.

Brunner, Emil. *The Misunderstanding of the Church*. 1950.

Caird, George. *Interpreter's Bible*. Vol. II. Abingdon Press.

Davies, J. G. *The Secular Use of Church Buildings*. 1968.

Dearmer, Percy. *The Parson's Handbook*. 7th Edition. Oxford University Press.

Forsyth, Cecil and Stanford, C. V. *History of Music*. Macmillan, 1916.

Jenkins, Daniel. *Christian Maturity and the Theology of Success*. SCM Press, 1976.

Lewis, C. S. *Christian Reflections*. Grand Rapids, Michigan: Eerdmans, 1971.

Maritain, J. *Art and Scholasticism*. Sheed and Ward, 1939.

Morris, Colin. *Include Me Out*.

Newman, Ernest. "Johann Sebastian Bach," ic *International Cyclopaedia of Music and Musicians*. Dent, 1942.

Oxford Dictionary of the Christian Church.

Robinson, J. A. T. *The New Reformation*.

Routley, Erik. *The Gift of Conversion*. Lutterworth Press, 1957.

———. *Twentieth Century Church Music.*, Oxford University Press, New York, 1965.

———. *Words, Music and the Church*. Abingdon Press, 1968.

Sayers, Dorothy. *The Mind of the Maker*. Methuen, 1941.
Scheide, William. *Johann Sebastian Bach as a Biblical Interpreter*. Princeton Pamphlets no. 8. Princeton, 1952.
Shaw, Martin. *The Principles of Church Music Composition*. SPCK 1921.
Smallman, Basil. *The Background of Passion Music*. SCM, 1957.
Evensong in Coventry Cathedral., compiled by Joseph W. Poole, 1971.

Index

Entries in SMALL CAPITALS refer to hymn tunes, in quotes, to hymns, in *italics*, to books or musical works

Forsyth, C., 69
Fundamentalism, musical, 25

Galatians 1.12, 18
  3.24, 21
  3–5, 17ff
Genesis 14, 13
  21.1ff, 18
Gerhardt, P., 42, 56
Golden Legend, The, 92
Gospel Songs, 135f
Goss, J., 124
Gounod, C., 61
Guitar, 106f

Handel, G. F., 59, 73
Haydn, J. M., 92
Hebrews 5.13f, 76
  12.2, 55
HELMSLEY, 74f
HEREFORD, 123
Hess, M., 59
Hitler, A., 46
Hora Novissima, 37
Howells, H., 45, 91
Hymn of Praise, 92
Hymns, accompaniment of, 102ff
Hymns Ancient and Modern, 75, 98

Interluding, 126
Introit, 126
Isaiah 1.12ff, 8
  5.1ff, 7
  5.11f, 9
  55.11, 86

Jazz, 89f
Jenkins, D. T., 2
Jeremiah 7.1ff, 8
John 6.15, 67
  6.22–7, 76, 85
  14–16, 95
John XXII, Pope, 69

Key in J. S. Bach, 52f
King's College (Cambridge), 47

Organ playing, 99ff
Organ Voluntary, 118f
Organum, 22
Oxford Movement, 71, 98

P. D. Q. Bach, 61
Pachelbel, J., 58
Palestrina, G. P. da, 51
Parry, C. H. H., 44f, 83
PASSION CHORALE, 42
Pergolesi, G., 43
Philippians 3.10ff, 66, 76
Piano in church, 106f
Pietism, 54ff
Pitch of hymns, 124
Pius IX, Pope, 106
Plainsong, 72
Poole, J. W., referred to as Precentor of Coventry: see Coventry
  Cathedral
Popular church music, 89
'Praise, my soul', 124
Processional hymns, 126
Prophets, O. T., 1ff
Prout, E., 60
Psalm tunes, Genevan and English, 73, 87
Psalms in worship, 117
Purcell, H., 33, 70, 73
Puritanism, 32

Rachmaninoff, S., 34, 52
Respighi, O., 60
Requiem (Verdi), 90
Revelation 11.15, 37
Ricercar, 72
Rippon, J., 71
Robinson, J. A. T., 65, 67
Romans 6.1ff, 66
  8.22, 37
Rossini, G., 43

Sacerdotalism, 116
SAGINA, 73f
St James's Church, Newcastle, 111, 144ff
ST MARY, 81
I Samuel 10, 1